BUT THEN AGAIN I COULD BE WRONG

THE BOOK OF RANTS

JIM RISING

 Tribute Books
Eynon, Pennsylvania

First Edition, November 2007

ISBN-13: 978-0-9795045-7-0
ISBN-10: 0-9795045-7-0

Published in the United States by
✳ Tribute Books
291 West Street, Eynon, PA 18403
(570) 876-2416 • tribute-books.com
SAN #256-4416

Author photo on back cover:
Guy Cali Associates, Clarks Summit, Pennsylvania

FOREWARNING

G ee...I always wanted to write a book. I never thought I would *but then again I could be wrong.* Here is a collection of some of the past few years "rants" as broadcast on WDMT 102.3 The Mountain as part of my show *Rising at Ten.*

You may notice some difference in quality, topicality and length. What you are seeing is a radio guy trying like hell to make sense on paper and it's been a long strange trip indeed. You will also notice that most of these are not "rants" in the sense that Dennis Miller takes on the world. They are called *Rising Rants* because of the alliteration. Thank God for spell checker or I would have butchered alliteration.

I need to let you know who to blame for this so I will list some of the people who made it their business to help me on this project. First and foremost would be Alan K. Stout, former editor of *The Weekender* where some of these "rants" have appeared over the past few years. Alan has been a constant source of inspiration and incredibly patient with my fledgling attempts at whatever it is I am doing here. Big thanks go out to current *Weekender* editor Rachel Pugh who continues to print my stuff, when I am sure there are massage parlor ads that could go in my space. Just a joke. I am kidding. Maybe not. I would be remiss to not mention Joe Butkiewicz who is Managing Editor at the *Times Leader,* who probably won't remember but who gave me words of wisdom when I first mentioned this idea to him. He said, "Write a bunch before you start running them."

How right you were, Joe. I need also to thank Nicole Langan owner of Tribute Books who gave me a great deal of help in getting this thing done and published. Nicole, your willingness to make this a worthwhile charity project by helping us to save some money on the printing is very much appreciated.

And speaking of that charity angle, thanks for purchasing this. All profits will go to the Hoyt Library in Kingston which lost its roof and much of its collection. I hope we can help put some books back on the shelves. Besides I figure they will feel guilty enough to put me on the same shelf with Salman Rushdie. I am kidding. Maybe not.

And last, but not least, I must thank the long suffering wife, Nancy, who is not named that for nothing. No one – and I mean no one – would have put up with me through the years and that's the truth. Thanks again for your support and as always thanks for listening.

Feel free to contact me via email at *rising@102themountain.com* if the spirit moves you. Write if you find work. Some copies of this book have $20 bills in them. Buy several to increase your chances of winning. Just kidding. Maybe not.

Jim Rising
October 2007

iv

All I wanted to do was fill the car up with overpriced gas.

W hy can't all the gas pumps be consistent when it comes to paying? Some say prepay, and some don't. In this day and age of petrol being as valuable as plutonium I understand that the temptation to pump and jump is greater then ever. So I understand that the service stations who suffer from this kind of theft sometimes want the cash in front. I have dealt with many transactions in my life that were cash in front and I have no big problem with that. The problem was that I did not know that I had to pay cash in front.

At 5 a.m. I was at the pump and even though that's pretty early I was alert enough to be able to read. So I did. I looked the pump over high and low and saw no sign that I was to pay first and pump later. To me that was sort of like a gift. Instead of walking in and handing over my cash and then walking back and pumping the gas and then walking back to get my change I could complete the transaction in one trip. But no. As soon as I squeezed the pump nozzle a harsh voice came out of some hidden speaker. "You have to prepay," it shouted. So I went in and gave the man my money.

Now I am sure the labor pool that gas stations have to draw upon for midnight to 6 a.m. workers is pretty shallow. But this guy looked like Festus from *Gunsmoke*. Only older. I remarked that there was no sign on the pump indicating prepay for cash. He said to me in the same voice that he used on the hidden speaker. "You have to prepay."

"I understand that," I said. "But you could put a sign on the pump and save us both time."

"You have to prepay" was his response.

At this point if my long suffering wife had been there with me she would have said, "Let it go." She wasn't and I couldn't. "I understand that you have to prepay," I said very slowly. "But why don't you put a sign on the pump that says that?"

"You have to prepay, too many drive-offs" was all I got this time.

So I gave Festus a $20 bill knowing it wouldn't fill my car but would get me away from there. Only it was not to be so simple. I put the nozzle on automatic and then went to try and scrape dead bugs off the windshield. When I heard the pump click off I heard those words again. "You have to prepay!"

Sure enough I checked the pump and for the first time in my lifetime the auto shut-off had failed. I owed 45 cents more. A lesser man might have cut and run. I went in with my dollar and paid up. And took one more run at it. "You really should put a sign up that says prepay," I said. Festus just looked at me and said....well you know what he said. *Or then again I could be wrong.*

Although my physique doesn't show it I have spent much of my adult life in one gym or another.

It's funny because as a kid in high school there was nothing I hated with a passion more than going to gym class. Every part of it was misery to me. It wasn't just that I hated physical exertion although that was a big part of it. I am not gifted in any way for any sport. To say that I throw a ball like a girl is demeaning to girls everywhere. I can't catch a ball to save my life or the many pairs of glasses that I have had broken trying to avoid being hit in the face. Hit a ball with a bat? It's to laugh. Run? Is there such an event as the 20 foot sprint? Because after 20 feet I am ready for the showers.

And that brings us to the next part of gym class I hated. The communal shower. Being out of shape all my life standing with all the other teen boys in the locker room was sheer hell. I admit that I have man breasts and if I didn't admit it the tough guys in the shower with me were certainly glad to point it out. Over and over again.

But as I grew up and became an even bigger adult I started working out in gyms. Working out is not like gym class in that it's mostly not competitive. It's also pretty safe for clumsy me as it's mostly machines that make it hard for me to drop things on my foot or someone else's.

And generally the locker rooms are equipped with private showers so the amount of time I have to show my shortcomings is thankfully brief. I say generally the showers are private but when I worked in Scranton there was this one gym where it was just like high school. Now this was a pretty upper crust gym. Why they let me in I have no idea but I was there sweating and straining with lawyers, judges and high powered businessmen. And we all paraded around each other lathered up in the little communal shower.

It was a little weird and I remember one time it got very weird. No, not that way, you pervert, but you aren't far off. I am in the shower when one other guy joins me. Of course guy etiquette in these circumstances dictates you don't look and don't talk. But as we rub and scrub I keep hearing this sound. It's metal on tile and it's coming from his side of the shower room.

Then I see it. I didn't want to but there it was. This guy had a not- so-small barbell in his special purpose. A piercing like through the top part, if you get my drift. Now I am a man of the world but I had never seen that before. I glanced at it and couldn't help it. I said "*ow.*"

He looked at me and smiled (alright this is already weird enough so stop with those thoughts) and said – and this is exactly what he said – "Yeah, it hurt at first but it was worth it. The ladies like it."

Yikes, I thought and then I said and this is exactly what I said "Oh." I think I changed gyms after shortly after that. *Or then again I could be wrong.*

And so I did it again.

A s my long suffering wife will readily admit, and she will tell almost anyone this, Mr. Home Handyman I am not. She also is ok with letting people know that I am not a fast learner. In fact it seems I don't really learn at all.

Last year in one of my early spring adventures in lawn care I got the Big Lawn Tractor stuck. It was a muddy place and I buried it up to the axles and got a small tree caught between the back wheel and the mowing deck. It was a two hour project to get the Big Lawn Tractor out that time and we were sure I could never be so stupid again. As usual we underestimated my stupid capacity.

Different place in the yard. No tree this time but the lawn tractor was acting like a pig in mud wallow. This time we are not so lucky. It is still there as I write this. It's been sinking further and further into the mud since Saturday. I really don't know how we will get it out this time.

I have tried shoveling a path for it but because it's sideways on a steep hillside it's not really working. Boards of all sorts of types, sizes and descriptions have been pushed under the rear tires in an effort to gain traction but no joy. I have completely disassembled the grass catcher to give better access to pushing but that didn't help and now the area around the mower looks like a yard sale with parts, shovels and boards scattered around the poor stuck beast. If it was a horse we might have shot it by now.

Suggested removal methods have included towing it out with a car or another mower. I don't have another mower (why would I?) and you can't get a car or truck into the area where I made my latest mistake. At a flea market at the Circle Drive-In, I looked at a hand powered winch, the kind my Dad would have called a come-a-long. I could clearly see myself attaching it to the mower, ratcheting the mechanism a few times and then deftly pulling the back end off the mower. Like I said, Mr. Home Handyman I am not. Even in my dreams.

Later on today my long suffering wife tells me we will get the Big Lawn Tractor out of its muddy prison. I hope she is right but I have my doubts. And I know the next step if we fail is to enlist the aid of my brother-in-law. I can hear him laughing already. *Or then again I could be wrong.*

Apparently my back yard is some sort of party central at night and I wasn't invited.

R ecently more than a foot of snow fell on our neck of the woods here at the Rising Ranch and it's more than a white nuisance to be plowed and shoveled out of our way. It's a detective tool that betrays the secret life of the woodsy creatures that I share this property with.

As I sit at my kitchen table writing this I can smell the stink of the Bengay I have rubbed into my sore muscles. Usually the long suffering wife does all the shoveling for me but since this storm fell on a weekend, I was handed my coat and gloves and shoved out the door. My back and my shoulders are in deep complaint over this.

But this morning in the bright new dawn, as I gaze out with less than pleasant thoughts about the nature of winter, I notice the surface of the snow has been disturbed by not a few but dozens of tracks. These weren't there yesterday as I slogged through the Arctic wasteland that is my domain.

Great circles and spirals across what would be in warmer months my lawn. "Deer," my long suffering wife says. But of course I need to go out and take a closer look. Sure enough she is right, mostly. The deer apparently were holding a square dance last night. What other explanation could there be for the random profusion and amazing number of the tracks. The explanation could be they were being chased by the neighbor's pesky Jack Russell terrors but the snow is too deep for that and in any case the only other tracks are not dog tracks.

But what a number and variety of tracks there are. These look like cat paws. Those over there must be squirrels and the tiny ones? Could they be mice? Or are they birds? Are those rabbit tracks?

While I had a long winter's nap warm and snug in my electric blanketed bed, the wildlife were having a wild time of it. I am sure that this probably happens all the time, but usually without the mantle of snow there is no incriminating evidence and the nocturnal culprits get away with it, scott free.

It's reassuring in a way that in spite of the below freezing temperatures and the unwelcome late March snow, life in these Pennsylvanian woods goes on. But still, might I be forgiven if I mutter under my breath, "Hurry spring." I know the weather guys say spring sprung last night. I don't think so. *But then again I might be wrong.*

*As a younger man I never ever even
glanced at the obituary page in a newspaper.*

O f course when you are young your concept of mortality is much less refined than it is when you are on the downward slope to the dirt nap. Now I check the notices of people who have died very carefully in case my name pops up. It would be just like me to die and not know about it. But so far, so good.

The other day I was looking at two recently departed and I couldn't help but wonder about the juxtaposition. The top obit was of a young girl who died before she reached her first birthday. The story told of a serious heart disease that claimed the infant before a transplant could be found.

Directly underneath this sadness was the story of a priest who lived to the ripe old age of ninety. No reason for his death was given and considering his advanced age, I guess none was needed.

What caught my eye were the photos of the two. The smile of the little girl is something to see. It seems to involve her whole face and I bet it wasn't the only smile she beamed out to the world in her short life. The priest also has a bright smile in the photo but the words written about his nearly fifty years of service as a priest were mostly just lists. They don't really give you a feel for his long life in service of others. But you can tell by looking at his face that he had seen many joyful things and many sad things as well, but they hadn't left him bitter or cynical.

Maybe it's a lot to infer from two grainy black and white pictures in a newspaper obituary. The two probably never met each other. The tiny girl seemed to have spent most of her life in hospitals, mainly in

Philadelphia. The priest was born in Nanticoke and died at his home in Mountain Top. But in spite of the fact that the two never crossed paths during the living years they are right next to each other in death on the page put together by some anonymous copy editor. I am willing to bet that the pairing was an accident, that no one else gave it a thought.

But there they are. A girl who didn't quite make it to six months and a priest who lived through two World Wars. Together forever on the page of a newspaper and if we are to believe the teachings of the old priest, together forever in another place as well. *Or then again I could be wrong.*

As I write this I am sitting at my kitchen table looking out at my back yard.

A ctually I can't see my back yard at all as it covered with at least two feet of snow. It's cold outside, well under freezing. The wind is blowing pretty hard so the wind chill must be very low, probably as low as my spirits are.

It's not that I don't understand the fact that we live in northeast Pennsylvania. It snows here and gets cold. But for much of this past winter we dodged the white stuff and the bone chilling cold. And now it seems all the worse for the time we spent in short sleeves earlier this winter. There was much talk about global warming and its effects on the climate when it was 50 degrees out in January. I don't hear a lot of that talk now. What I hear are the sounds of snowplows scraping by on the road and the muted roar of my furnace burning dollar bills.

My preference when I am at my leisure at my house is to wear t-shirts. Today I have one on. It's under the sweater and the flannel shirt. My hands are not as cold as they were yesterday when I tried to scrape the frozen crap off my car windshield but it's not what I would call tropical here in the Rising Ranch.

Because we went from having no snow to Arctic-like cold for the first year in the 25 years we have lived in this house, the water pipes froze. You haven't lived until you have tried to unthaw the pipes using a small electric heater. It's just short of futile but no way is the call to the plumber going to be made on my watch. And now that I have the water running again we are leaving the kitchen sink run a few drips all the time. That's not too annoying.

I won't even mention the day the garage door froze shut. And the day the man who plows the driveway got half of it done and then just gave up. "Too much snow," he said.

And so I look for signs, any sort of omen that spring will soon be here. I grasp at any positive news and I have a little to share. It must be near the end of winter and the beginning of spring if Jones Potato Pancakes stand on Harvey's Lake is open. And they are. Just on the weekends, mind you. But Friday, Saturday and Sunday you can have a little taste of summer. Call 570-639-5243 to order ahead. It's just a small sign, but hopeful nonetheless. *Or then again I could be wrong.*

It's been a long time since I have bounced a check.

B ut in my lifetime of banking fun, I have had more than one or two of mine go all flubber and act like they were on little financial trampolines. I used to wonder how banks made so much money but after a few insufficient funds fees I know for sure. But evidently it's worse than you or I even knew.

The check bouncing business is big business for your local friendly banker and they have even found a way to maximize their profits. It's something called high to low check processing and it works like this.

Say you have $100 in your account. You write checks for $25, $50, $17 and $95. The bank will cash the $95 one first. If they had gone in the order you wrote the checks you would have still occurred a bounced check fee but only one instead of three. Fair? Of course not. But that's the way the check bounces.

The banks of course smugly say that they are looking out for the customer's best interest in cashing the big checks first. Their contention is that you would rather bounce a few checks and pay more in fees than bounce the mortgage check. My contention is that Scrooge is alive and well and laughing all the way to the bank.

When those bounced checks fees start to pile up and you are trying to explain to Guido, the enforcer, why your car payment went all rubber, it's not too much comfort to know that your six dollar check to the beer store was cashed ok.

A while ago an acquaintance of mine who lives down south told me he had been locked up for bouncing a check. The thing was the check was over two years old. The cops barged into his office, put him in cuffs and slapped him behind bars with no warning or chance to clear the check. He ended up in court and after paying a lawyer more than the check was worth he was let off with a hefty fine and a permanent stiff neck from watching his back.

And don't get me started on the lag time between making a deposit and the money actually showing up in your account. You can deposit a check written from an account held by the bank you are doing business with and still wait three days for it to show up in your account. Meanwhile, good old Guido is knocking on your door with brass knuckles. The old saying goes something like "The rich get richer." *And then again I could be wrong.*

Can we unlatch ourselves from a goal driven life?

W hy is it that we always seem to be working for more stuff? A better car, bigger house, a vacation home? Are we just wired that way, or is it something we have learned and having learned it, can we unlearn it?

I have seen this in my own life quite often. I will really want something, let's say a sports car. I will work and save and beat down the objections of my long suffering wife and finally I get the thing. Now I don't want to say for even minute that I don't love and cherish my little car. But it somehow seems that the wanting was a much stronger emotion than the having. It's sort of like, now what? The answer is in there somewhere.

The happiness of the little sports car was in the pursuit. I spent literally years seeking out the perfect-for-me car. I logged countless hours on the computer, learning about the type of car I wanted. I searched eBay and other sites trying to find the perfect one in my price range. I must have looked at fifty or more of these cars in the area and even while on vacation. "Wait honey, pull over- there's one in that farmer's field. It might run. Is that a tree growing out of the hood?"

So if a material achievement leaves you happy for only a short while, why do we keep going after the next goal? Lately I have found myself looking at other sports cars. Wouldn't it be great if I had a Corvette? My long suffering wife just shakes her head and sighs.

Sometimes it seems like this is a sort of like being on a treadmill. I always wanted a house. I got a house. Now I want a bigger house. Or I want a house by a lake. But taking care of the house I have and making my mortgage payments makes the dream of that other house a real stretch. But maybe if we work and save and do without and make ourselves miserable in the process, maybe we can find that bigger house. But when we get there, will the same thing happen again? The best advice I have heard is choose your treadmills with care. You will be on them for a long time. *Or then again I could be wrong.*

I don't spend too much time in greeting card stores.

Like most men I have only a few occasions that I must get cards for – birthday, anniversary, Christmas….I think that's about it. Oh, Valentine's Day. I was in the card store for the anniversary reason the other day. It's clear to me that card stores are designed by and for members of the fairer sex. The reason I am so confident in this fact is that I have never seen another guy in a card store other than Valentine's Day or around Christmas. Just not a place we men hang out.

Other clues are everywhere. Not to be sexist but the style and sentiments of most cards are not exactly dripping with testosterone. Not too many cards with pictures of tanks and machine guns, if you get my drift.

The other thing I noticed about card stores is the truly disturbing variety of events you can find a card for. Not only can you find sympathy cards for the loss of a beloved pet, you can find cards for specific types of pets. Dog? Cat? Horse? Monkey? It's all there in the card store. There are cards for people coming out of rehab. Cards for people going into rehab. I think I saw a card for a person who needs to go to rehab. Cards for graduation (and most of these have a handy pocket for cash) for every grade from pre-school to grad school.

And the dead giveaway to me that card stores are female orientated? Cards for no good reason at all. It even says so on the card rack thingy. Cards, just because. I know that there is not a man in the northeastern Pennsylvania area that has ever sent a card for no reason at all. There's always a motive for a guy to send a card, and it's usually centered around…well I don't need to spell it out, right?

Card stores designed by and for men would be somewhat different. First of all they would have only cards for the big occasions I mentioned before, anniversary, birthday, Christmas and …what was the other one….? Oh, Valentine's Day. The cards would be in racks where the price would be displayed clearly and would relate only to the size of the card. In a guy's card store the bigger the card, the better. Guys don't buy small cards. Big card good. And finally all the sentiments would be exactly the same. Happy_____fill in the blank. I love you. Now can we go to bed? I think I am on to something. Gotta come up with a catchy name for the guy's card store. Maybe combine two stores. That's it. Beer and cards. Beercardo? *Or then again I could be wrong.*

It's a rare motorist in Northeast Pennsylvania who hasn't had an encounter with a deer.

I f you haven't actually had the misfortune of plowing into one of the four legged critters then someone close to you has. I know people who have hit deer on the way to the body shop to get damage caused by hitting a deer fixed. I am beginning to believe that the body shop owners of northeast Pennsylvania have a deal with the deer. What else can explain the deer's single-minded mission to wait until the last possible moment to cross the road? I don't know what the guys who bend fenders for a living have over the deer but it must be some powerful voodoo to make them jump happily in front of big SUVs.

In past years I lived in New England, rural Vermont for God's sake and never hit a deer, nor did I know anyone who did. According to various insurance companies we here in northeast Pennsylvania hit more deer than any other state. We're number one! And this is the time of year where we rack (no pun intended) up most of the kills. The deer are in the mating season and so have more on their little minds then looking both ways before they cross.

I have had the experience of deer meeting bumper only once. It was on the Pennsylvania Turnpike and I may have been exceeding posted speed limits. But this deer literally appeared out of nowhere.

The area I was traveling through was bordered on one side by a wide open field. The other side had steep rocky cliffs. Now I know that the deer didn't come from the field side. I am sure I would have seen it and been able to make evasive maneuvers. What must have happened is the animal fell off the cliff into the path of my car. In any case it happened so fast it was like a magic trick.

I was driving along digging the tunes on my radio and next thing I knew, bang there was a deer head on my hood. The impact must have cut the critter in a few parts and the head landed first on the hood and then slammed with great force onto my windshield. It was more than the wipers could handle that's for sure.

In the words of the body shop guy, "You were lucky you didn't get that head in your lap."

I didn't exactly feel lucky and the total bill to repair my car definitely didn't make me feel like going right out and renting the movie *Bambi*. *Or then again I could be wrong.*

You've probably seen the ads.

R ecently the Department of Transportation has been playing an $11 million campaign on TV and the internet in an effort to curb drunk driving. *Drunk driving. Over the limit. Under arrest.* The campaign shows cops pulling over guys in cars filled with beer, wine and liquor. Not bottles. Cars filled to the windows with booze. It's pretty startling to see and it makes the point pretty clear. The tag line is "Make no mistake: You will get caught, you will be arrested."

Nationwide deaths from drunk driving make this problem seem like a mini holocaust. In 2005, nearly 17,000 lost their lives at the hands of some drunk fool behind the wheel of a car. That's roughly the amount of people that would attend two sold-out shows at Wachovia Arena.

By the way, in terms of national ranking Pennsylvania tips the bar at number four with 636 deaths in 2005, actually up from 616 in 2004. The only states with more booze-induced fatalities are California, Texas and Florida so obviously we are doing something wrong. Even New York State which you would figure to have a high number throws away about 100 fewer lives each year.

How could we lower the number of gravestones planted in honor of over consumption? I think we could take a page from the old mining towns. If you ask an old timer what life was like when coal was king here, you'll get a lot of answers. One that always foams to the top is the fact that every block had a church, a corpse house and two or three beer gardens. You would never drive to any of the watering holes back then. After your shift in the mines, you would cut the dust and then some at the neighborhood beer garden and then stagger home under your own power.

I don't have any way of gathering statistics of deaths from drunk walking back then, but common sense tells us it was probably negligible. The consequences of over consumption were probably no less severe when you arrived home via shank's mare (picture housewife with rolling pin at the door as a greeting) but at least you weren't in a pile of twisted wreckage by the side of the road. I am not advocating more drinking but I am in favor of a bar near every house. More jobs, more businesses and fresher beer for everyone. Better yet: door to door deliveries. Just like the milkman only different. *Or then again I could be wrong.*

*During the holiday season, the number
of stupid drivers increases by a factor
that I can't begin to calculate.*

M ath is not my strong suit but I can tell you this. If every other driver isn't brain dead on the highways then it's every third one. I have seen driving behaviors that just plain defy any logic.

The other day we were in the long line for the right turn that leads off the Cross Valley to the Wyoming Valley Mall. It's always backed up and this time of year it moves like molasses on a cold January day. The left turn lane is by comparison always fairly clear. So is that why people in locomotive-sized SUVs insist on driving supersonic speeds in that lane? Because everyone else is moving at a snails pace and they can floor it, they do? God forbid the accident that will occur if you open your car door to spit.

And what happened to the nursery school rule about no cutting in line? At the end of the off ramp there is always some idiot who is the left hand lane trying to cut over. He or she has skipped the whole long line and now wants to bully their way in. And what amazes me more is some people let them. This is why cars don't have bumper-mounted machine guns. The loss of life would be enormous.

And don't get me started about cell phone usage behind the wheel. You are in charge of a speeding SUV with four or nine passengers inside. Some of the riders are young children. Some of them are crying or carrying on in a distracting manner. Traffic is heavy and you have one hand on the wheel and the other is holding the cell phone up to your ear so you can chat. You are an accident waiting to happen.

Five states have banned the use of handheld cell phones while driving. Not here in the good old Commonwealth of Pennsylvania. Feel free to discuss what's for dinner while paying only marginal attention to the three ton vehicle you are driving 20 miles per hour over the posted speed limit.

I strongly feel they should sell cell phones with a skull and cross bones on the face plate and a warning like on cigarette packs. Something like, "If you are so stupid as to use this behind the wheel you deserve a painful death and we hope you don't kill anyone else."

My hope is that when dead drivers are asked by St. Peter if they were on a cell phone when they plowed into the school bus that they get dispatched to the circle of hell where Adolph Hitler, Saddam Hussein and Idi Amin are entertainment directors. *Or then again I could be wrong.*

Every person I have told this to thinks I am a little nuts.

W ell that's no surprise is it? But what I am about to tell you, and I swear it's the God's honest truth, is so strange and bizarre that most people when they hear it, they just sort of edge away. This is a real conversation stopper and always gets me the look like I have sprouted another head.

I am having a problem with time. No, it's not the usual problem which is there is not enough of it. My problem is that time seems to be playing games with me. Time is an interesting concept. I was once told that the real reason for time was so that everything didn't happen at once. Stephen Hawking wrote an entire book about it called *A Brief History of Time*. It's not particularly brief and it's pretty tough to digest for a simple man such as myself.

Different people may judge identical lengths of time quite differently. Time can "fly" that is; a long period of time can seem to go by very quickly. Times that "fly" almost never seem to happen at work. Likewise, time can seem to "drag," as in when one performs a boring task. Time always seems to "drag" at work.

The perceived speed of time depends on a number of factors. If a person has a very long list of things to do on a certain day like say a "Honey do" list, the day may feel like it has not enough hours to do everything. Likewise, even a short wait at the dentist can feel endless. A day filled with fun activities can feel very long due to the number of activities that fill it. A long trip can go by quickly if the traveler's mind is occupied or if you drive well above the posted speed limit. Unless you meet a state trooper who has a differing opinion.

Time also seems to go fast when sleeping. And that's where my problem comes about. Not when I am sleeping. When I stop sleeping. I wake up fairly often during the night. Sometimes two or three times a night. Old age, full bladder...my problem is that when I wake up and look over at my digital clock it often – and I mean like almost every time – is reading 1:11 or 2:22 or 3:33 or (and this one is real often) 4:44. No kidding. Anybody have any clues about this? It's starting to freak me out a little. I think I am going to get rid of the digital clock and get an old fashioned one with hands. *Or then again I could be wrong.*

Few people know who Albert Payson Terhune was.

M ore might be familiar with the book – *Lad a Dog*. Terhune, who lived from 1872 to 1942, wrote a series of books about Lad, a rough Collie and his offspring and their adventures in a place called "Sunnybank."

As it turns out Sunnybank is a real place in a town called Pompton Lakes, New Jersey. I know more about this than most as I have been a visitor to the site of Sunnybank for the past few years. Even though the town of Pompton Lakes in a fit shortsightedness bulldozed the Sunnybank home of Terhune and his dogs in 1969, the lovers of Collies still gather there a few times a year to celebrate all that is Collie.

My oblique membership in this clan is by marriage. My long suffering wife's sister is a Collie lover with no fewer than three of the long haired rascals in residence at her home at anytime. Sunnybank is therefore somewhat like Mecca to her and I have learned that a happy sister-in-law makes for a happier wife so we go.

The "gatherings" at Sunnybank are a dog show exclusive to Collies. Lassie would feel right at home there as it is infested with Collies of every size, shape, hue and age. The dogs, particularly the puppies, are undeniably cute, but to a non-dog person after a while it becomes a bit predictable, not to say boring but hey if you have seen one mess of cute-as-a-button Collie pups barking and wagging you have seen them all.

But no complaint. I learned some neat new usages of words during some of the seminars on Collie breeding during this summer's visit. The first time I heard the man holding the little puppy up say, "this little bitch," I was somewhat taken aback. I was reminded by my wife that a bitch is what they call a female dog. I said, "I'll say," but I don't think my remark went over well. Then the puppy man started saying "damn" over and over again. I was told that "dam" also refers to a female Collie but I am not so sure the little puppy hadn't leaked on him. Then he started talking about pricks, but he was pointing at the puppy's ears so I guess he meant those. Walking out of the puppy show, I encountered a woman who claimed to have a girl Collie who was due to be a mommy Collie any day. She looked right at me and proudly said, "There are two in the bitch right now." I hardly knew how to respond. *But then again I could be wrong.*

***Four years seems both like an eternity
and like the blink of an eye.***

O ne thousand four hundred and sixty one days ago, the whole way we look at the world as Americans changed. Before 9/11 there were plenty of reasons to know that segments of the planet were populated by people who hate our very existence. The bombings and attacks on embassies and military targets. Even the first World Trade Center bombing should have been enough to let us know that evil lurks out there and it has as its target – us. But somehow when those planes driven by madmen crashed into the World Trade Center, the Pentagon and the ground in Somerset County here in Pennsylvania, a little of the American spirit crashed with them.

We had lived for so many years with the knowledge, now shown to be false, that it can't happen here. Somehow we forgot that being the biggest, the strongest and the best also made us the biggest target. Now we know. As always happens the mist of time passing has softened the blow, has healed the scars and we have moved on. But we will never be the same as we were four years ago.

Talking about it over the weekend brought back the memories, the emotion and the feeling of helplessness and the anger at that helplessness. Four years is a long time in anybody's life. I have seen the deaths of loved ones, the marriage of my children and so many other changes in my life that it seems like a blur. When I think about how profoundly the lives of those who had loved ones taken by the savages have been affected I know my little troubles are insignificant indeed.

In the weeks and months directly after 9/11 we all showed our flags, we all pitched in and we all stood fast as Americans. The same cannot be said now. And so in the final analysis what have we learned? Is it only in crisis, like 9/11 and the relief efforts for the victims of Hurricane Katrina that we act as one? It's not a great question. But maybe it needs to be asked.

In case we ever forget.

I t's been four years since the barbarians from the East showed us their asses and did the cowardly deeds that resulted in a changed world for all. There are 1,152 victims of the World Trade Center bombing whose remains have never been found.

Now on the roof of the building next door at 130 Liberty Street, the former Deutsche Bank building, workers who are getting set to tear down the structure have found what have been positively identified as human bone fragments. Ten small pieces of bone ranging from half an inch to about two inches, some perhaps from a rib cage have been turned over to the medical examiners office. The fragments are large enough and in such condition that the medical examiners are confident they can extract DNA samples and may be able to get some profiles.

The building's roof was 800 feet under the south tower and was wrecked by debris from the collapse and even though it is still standing it has never been reopened. The Kirby Center would fit 1,152 people comfortably. In case we ever forget.

He – or maybe it was she, I can never tell – was singing so loud.

I t sounded like it was on my head or had landed on my shoulder. It was my first robin of the year and there was no missing it. I looked around but at first I couldn't spot it.

The place where I work is what I would consider a bad place for wildlife of any sort. Next to our offices is a car dealer on the one side and a motel that has seen better years. On the other side are four lane highways, certain death for anything not in a car and for many who are. It's a busy noisy exhaust smelling place and not the place where one expects to see the harbinger of spring, but there it was. Singing its brains out. It must be a boy robin seeking a mate. Why else would it be trilling and soloing like Louie Armstrong on meth?

I stopped in my journey to the office door and another day of tilting at radio windmills and looked and looked some more. Finally I spotted him, on the highest branch of a bush next to the driveway. The only patch resembling Mother Nature in this mess of asphalt and automobiles and there he was.

I watched him for a minute or two and saw his tiny beak open and close as he sang his song. What he lacked in rhythm and harmony, he made up for with sheer volume and enthusiasm. It seemed like he puffed up a little with each section of his free form composition. Definitely showing off for the girl robins.

I watched him for a few minutes more and then made my way into another day that had nothing to do with robins or showing off for girls. That night as I made good my escape for the day, I had forgotten completely about the bird on the bush and wasn't reminded of him until the next morning when he was back in the same place and so was I. In fact, the loud bird was there every day last week. Singing its little birdie heart out.

I know that I have said it must be in an effort to find a mate, but I can't help but feel that there must be some joy in the act of making such a gleeful noise. I won't be too surprised if he lands a mate. There seems to be a bumper crop of robins this year. I am glad they are back. It must be a sign that summer and warm days are near, right? *Or then again I could be wrong.*

Help me figure this one out.

R ecently a 19-year-old woman named Sara broke into a house in Kingston, Pennsylvania and stole a can filled with coins. She actually didn't break in – she crawled through a dog door. I am guessing Sara is not overweight. She is also a drug addict because she was charged with possession of a controlled substance.

I noticed this in the *Citizens Voice*. It was the top item in the local news section. Right underneath was the story of Ken from Brooklyn. Police caught him at a home on North Meade Street with a bunch of crack cocaine, a 45 caliber semi automatic handgun and almost $1,200 in cash. Ken was trying to flush the stash down the toilet when they busted him. Ken will spend the next one to two years as our guest in the Luzerne County Correctional Facility. We will clothe him, feed him, give him medical and dental care and try to rehabilitate him.

Sara was deported. The judge told her not to come back to Luzerne County. Time served. Leave. Don't darken our doggie doors again.

So the guy who was obviously big trouble gets a two year vacation on us. I know prison is not vacation but you know what I mean. He gets to stay here and when released is free to go back to North Meade Street with his crack and his gun and his intent to commit harm to local folks with his poison.

The girl who is in big trouble, and not to mention probably could use a decent meal, gets the boot. Am I missing something here, or what?

Hi, my name is Jim and I am an email addict.

The room says, "Hi, Jim!" This is my story. It started off innocently enough. I got AOL on my lumbering 286. I didn't use it too often in those early days. You had to get your connection and that was time consuming. And you paid your connection by the minute. *Ouch!* But still the sound of that voice got its hooks into me. *You've got mail. Wow!* What a rush it was.

Then came the day I moved on to an actual ISP. My connection of choice was Epix and even though it was still dial-up I was using a couple of hours a day. Spam was still in the kitchen cupboard.

Then came the day I started using email at work. All of a sudden I was checking my email two, three, sometimes even four times a day! One day I even found myself sending an email to the person in the office next to me. What was wrong with me?

Soon I had an email monkey on my back. I set my desktop computer up so I could check all of my email accounts constantly. By now I had five email addresses. And by this time the emails were all being cut with spam. To get to the good stuff you had to sort through all the seeds and stems of that junk. The inbox was consuming my life. And I was powerless to stop.

Soon the connections both at work and at home got faster and better. Now I was mainlining email at home with DSL. It made the old dial-up stuff seem like drinking warm water. This was so intoxicating that I spent more time on email than I did anything else.

I had computers in every place I went. Wireless laptops hidden around the house so I could get my fix. I knew that I was hitting rock bottom when I got my Blackberry. Now I could check my email anywhere. It's shameful to me now to admit the places that I logged on. I was in agony when the network went down. How could I live without my connection? When I found myself answering an email while I was on the toilet I knew it was time to come here, to the rooms of E.M.A.A. Email Addicts Anonymous. I had hit rock bottom.

The road to recovery is slow. All around me are the temptations to log on and get a quick email fix. I know that I have a long way to go but I have hope. You can too. Just remember. One email at a time. By the way. Can someone email me when the next meeting is? *Or then again I could be wrong.*

I am always and forever a student of humans.

Having been one myself for more decades than I care to admit I find our situations very comical sometimes. If you can't laugh then you have to cry and I would prefer to wear in the laugh lines a bit more.

The other night at a restaurant the man two booths down was clearly choking. He was barking like a seal and his wife (I assume..a date wouldn't have yelled at him quite this way) was yelling at him to take small bites and slow down or else she would have to perform the "Heineken" maneuver on him. I got to laughing so hard that my wife yelled at me.

I bought gas at one of the mega huge stations the other day. Filled my car up which cost $18.70. Went in and got a soda and stood in line. Guy in front of me was having some trouble with his transaction. The confusion seemed to be they thought he hadn't paid. He was sure he had and he knew this because...how? He had given them $40 in advance and pumped only $30. He wanted his $10 back and they at the counter were not budging an inch.

I wasn't in a hurry so I just watched. It took 10 minutes and three levels of managers to get the man his double sawbuck back. Now it's my turn. Remember the $18.70 in gas? Add a soda in (has to be at least a buck, right?) and hand them a $20. Get $5 and change back. I stood there and looked at the bill, looked at the girl behind the counter. I was blocking the next customer. Finally I said (and I hope I am always this honest), "Excuse me, I think I owe you money."

"No," she said.

They gathered the three managers again – you have to wonder how many times this happens – and

assured me I was fully paid. I went back to the pump –
sure that I was getting too old to handle this stuff – when
before my wondering eyes, the pump did read $18.70.
Back in the door, waited again and tried once more to do
the right thing. No dice. I was mistaken. So if the guys at
the Sheetz across from the Wal-Mart/Sam's Club in
Wilkes-Barre, Pennsylvania want the difference, write
me an e-mail.

I am in cell hell.

A while back I gave up my "CrackBerry" for a regular cell phone. This made me sad, but I took it like a man. Or course I had to hand transfer the six million phone numbers in my phone, but so what?

Then my company changed cell phone providers. Of course this meant I would be changing phones for the third time in as many months. The nice salesman came up with a phone with slide-out keyboard about the size of a bass harmonica. In go my 10 million phone numbers.

Then I discovered the phone had no signal in my house. I whined and begged and pleaded like a kid to my boss who finally gave in and allowed to me to move to yet another carrier, one that would work in my kitchen. This means, if you are counting, four phones that I have entered all my 20 million phone numbers in less than four months. My fingers are healing up quite nicely, thanks for caring.

But now the third circle of cell hell begins. This new cell company sold me on a phone that rhymes with GEO. This phone is a joke. They built three of this model phone, two blew up at the factory injuring several workers and the third one is mine. You can't get it to dial the right number half the time. The worst part of this phone from hell is that it dials by itself. I have been told by almost everyone in my address book that they have heard from me when I haven't called then in months.

The other day was the last straw. I was in the gym at 5 a.m. The phone was in my gym bag. I kept hearing this tiny voice sounding very upset. It finally screamed, "Jimmy," loud enough for me to hear. Now there are only three people who have ever called me Jimmy. Two of them are dead now, so I knew it had to be my sister in

Vermont. I lunged for the phone and – you guessed it – hung up on my sister. I frantically dialed her back, calling three other people in the process. Remember it's 5 a.m. When I did get her, it's busy. Of course. She was waking up my long suffering wife. I called home and my none-too-pleased wife said, "What's wrong? Your sister is on call waiting and she doesn't understand why you called her and then wouldn't talk to her." I want my "CrackBerry" back. If the boss refuses I wonder how he will like those 5 a.m. wake up calls? *Or then again I could be wrong.*

I am not really that hard to please.

A t least I don't think I am. But I cannot understand for the life of me why the fast food order window always gets it wrong. Now don't get me wrong – I make mistakes in my job. Lots of them. The other day I thought I erased an entire database. It turns out I was wrong which proves I can make a mistake, right?

Back to the fast food order window. I order the same lunch every day. A chicken sandwich, hold the sauce. A small salad, no dressing. An ice tea, with fake sweetener and no lemon. They always ask if I want lemon. I always say no. I almost always get lemon in my tea. I have my own dressing. They always ask. I always decline. I always get a packet. I always specify I want none of the horrid sauce. About every other time I get gobs of the yucky stuff.

Oh and with that iced tea? First of all the size without asking can be wildly different. The other day, much to my surprise I got what looked like a bucket with a straw in it. One time I got a cup that held..well about a cup's worth. And can they spare the sweetener? Either I get none (usually) or one or two. Try sweetening a bucket of ice tea with two of those packets.

Now I realize in the great scheme of the universe that my problem is very small. But think of this. I get this experience every time. Multiply my wrong order by the billions and billions of wrong orders there must be. It's gotta cost someone something somewhere, don't you think? Never mind the cost in anger and spoiled salad dressing. *But then again I could be wrong.*

I am not what you would call a seasoned air traveler.

I fly only when I have to and then only with great reluctance. Picture someone trying to lead a mule someplace where the mule does not want to go. That mule would be me at the boarding gate.

Although in recent years I have had to become somewhat better at getting on one of those steel tubes, I will never love it. Recent events have done nothing to change my mind.

A while back I had to fly on business. As is customary in these days of air travel out of the Wilkes-Barre/Scranton International School of Airports and truck driving you can't get there from here and you have to go somewhere else in between. So instead of making one plane flight, one take-off and one landing, you get to have the fun and excitement of – for me anyway – defying gravity and certain death four times. Two holding my breath take-offs and two white knuckle landings.

We made the up and down of the first one without incident other than me turning somewhat blue on the take-off. If I don't hold my breath the plane will not have enough power to make it up into the wild blue yonder and it had been a while since I had flown so I was out of practice.

It was the second leg of the journey where we had a little trouble. As we sat all seat-belted in, waiting for the push back from the gate, the captain came over the intercom with his NASA sounding pilot's voice. "Well, ladies and gentlemen the ground crew has noticed a little hydraulic fluid on the ground near the wings so they are going to take a closer look at the problem. We should be underway real soon."

I began to panic in a quiet way but held my ground. Twenty or so minutes passed before we heard from the cockpit again and it wasn't good news. The pilot said, and this is exactly what he said, "I am sorry to have to tell you that the hydraulic fluid from the wing means the stabilizer won't work right so this plane is cooked. We are looking for another aircraft so you need to get off the plane and wait in the boarding area for further information."

Wait in the boarding area? The plane is COOKED? I made a beeline for the nearest place dispensing liquid courage and had several helpings. As you can tell I made it back in one piece but I will never forget the pilot's words. I am almost sure telling the passengers that a plane is cooked is not in the airlines' approved manual of things to say from the cockpit, *but then again I could be wrong.*

I am overdue for a haircut.

I come from a generation that considered long hair much more than just a fashion statement. It was a clear defining mark of who you were and what you believed in.

All my teen life I fought with my parents, unsuccessfully, to get my hair to the length I thought it should be. Just when I got it to be good in the back, I was marched off the barber shop. No fancy hair stylist for me. I went to the same guy who gave me a scundy when I was 11-years-old.

If your hair was too short, you were a straight or worse yet a nark and even though I could have stepped over mounds of drugs and not known what they were I certainly didn't want to appear uncool.

And so it was that my graduation picture from high school shows me with white sidewalls and not much on top. When I left to go to the big city for college of course the first two things I did was let my hair go without any scissor action and to grow a beard. When I returned home my mom had added long hair and a beard to the graduation picture.

Nowadays I am only too glad to keep my hair short. In fact I wish I had the testicular fortitude to just shave it all off. It's a pain in the rear to take care of when it gets too long and wearing headphones or windy days make me look like a rooster.

I am ashamed to admit that a few years back I actually had my hair colored. The occasion was my daughter's wedding and I thought I would impress the ex-wife and her kin with my youthful appearance.

It was a disaster. I went, on the recommendation of one of our sales staff, to what I was assured was the best such place to have it done. My hair is normally mouse-colored these days. A little brownish blondish but mostly grey. The hair folks gave me a treatment, I went home and looked in the mirror and saw Bozo the Clown looking back. It wasn't just reddish. It was hunter blaze orange. I looked like a traffic cone. I went back to the salon and they frowned at me and tried again. This time I looked like the famous red-headed stepchild.

Needless to say I am not a big fan of hair coloring. I guess I earned the grey so I will keep it. And unless I miss my guess, I didn't make too much of an impression on the ex. The big lesson, of course, was to not care.

I am pretty sure the annual trek to
the mall area is over with for this year.

I am of course talking about Christmas shopping which for me is almost but not quite as pleasurable as having a root canal done without anesthesia by a drunken sadistic dentist.

First there are the drivers who only venture out this time of year. Oh, of course, there are stupid motorists on the roadways of northeast Pennsylvania all seasons of the year but the holidays bring them out in packs.

The latest trick of these once-a-year road nuisances is the traffic light surprise. Apparently the concept of green means go takes awhile to register this time of the season. Over the weekend I sat behind at least five drivers who just didn't move when the light turned green. At first I waited 15 to 20 seconds before tapping my horn. Later on in the day when my patience was all gone, it didn't take that long before I leaned on the honker quite a bit faster. Like maybe a second.

Then there is the Parking Space Olympics. The game begins when you see someone get in their car. You wait for them to vacate the space and then you have a space, right? Oh, if life was only that simple. First of all, the estimated time it takes someone to actually move out of the space is measured best by using a calendar. Usually by this time, a line of cars has appeared behind you, some of them honking at you to get out of the way. Then chances are about 50/50 someone in the opposite direction will zoom in the space while the person is backing out. I have seen a homicide committed over this.

Now you are actually in the store. The long suffering wife is always well equipped with a list and a clear sense of purpose of what she wants. But she is also possessed (and I use that word with no reference to Linda Blair) with an unshakable idea that everyone on our list needs to get the same amount of gifts. This means many last minute agonized decisions about what to get someone to even it up.

This is where many stores make out like bandits as frantic husbands grab anything on the shelf and say, "What about this?" The "this" in question of course may be a bag of kitty litter but it seems like a good idea at the time.

Also, and not to be unkind but many of the other shoppers appear to have come from other planets. There are hair styles and clothing matches that make you wonder if they had any mirrors in the house before they ventured out. In the words of Andy Williams: "It's the holiday season/With the whoop-de-do and hickory dock/And don't forget to hang up your sock." *Or then again I could be wrong.*

I am the clumsiest person I know.

M y long suffering wife will vouch for this. If dropping things ever becomes an Olympic event I will take home the gold medal except, of course, I will drop it.

My life is a constant blur of trips, slips and falls. I spill stuff, break things and hurt myself 10 times a day. And that's on a good day. I have no item of clothing that hasn't had at least a meal's worth of spills on it. I once spilled something I was eating on my shirt, changed into a new one and immediately spilled the same thing again within seconds. I don't own a tie that doesn't have the remains of some meal on it. I drop food on the floor and then slip on it trying to clean it up. The other day I spilled a bottle of pills. Over a hundred pills scattered all over the kitchen floor. We'll be finding them for months.

I love to cook, but when I am done the long suffering wife must spend hours scrubbing every surface in the kitchen and sweeping the floor of all my droppings.

I consider myself a good driver but if there is a pothole within five states of where I am driving, I will hit it dead center. The guys who align my car just sigh.

I have given up trying to be Mr. Home Handyman around the Rising Ranch. It's not that I don't want to do things but how many times can I get the lawn tractor stuck before I learn not to drive it into the wet places on the lawn. The answer is I always find new wet spots. The last time – and I do mean the last time – I climbed a ladder I fell so hard that I left a dent in the concrete floor of the garage. I tried to change the spool of cord on my lawn trimmer once. I ended up buying a new one. I own a chain saw. I will confess I am terrified to use it. Even if I manage not to cut my leg off, I know I will drop a tree on my house or get the saw stuck in a log.

As a result of this congenital clumsiness I have become very careful about walking. Especially now with the ice and snow I move like I am made out of bone china. It does no good. The other day I fell in a perfect imitation of a *Three Stooges* bit. If I was being scored even the Russian judges would have awarded me 10s across the board. *Or then again I could be wrong.*

I gave up coffee a while ago.

I just stopped cold turkey one day and switched over to tea. There were a number of reasons for this. I noticed that my consumption of coffee was keeping pace with the number of antacid tablets I was chewing down. When I got up to a bottle of Tums a week I figured that was a message. We won't go into the other reason in detail but suffice it to say I was regular customer at the stall on the right in the men's room and leave it at that.

I found a tea with twice as much caffeine as coffee so I am still getting my morning jolt. I just am not getting the sour stomach.

I was a manly coffee drinker. The place where I work has free coffee and the fixings come in little bags. One bag per pot is the idea. When I made the brew I would put at least one and a half bags in. We even had a code for this strong brew, calling it a one dot five pot. Of course as the first, strongest part of the coffee dripped out like sludge my cup would be under the spout to catch it so I got the strongest part of these strong pots. And oh yes. I drank it black as the interior of my soul. And I drank gallons of it.

But that was then and this is now and what does my wondering eye notice but a new coffee designed for people who still want the java but have sensitive stomachs. Folgers is marketing the stuff, calling it "simply smooth." The ad campaign reads, "The return of the second cup."

The problem as Folgers sees it is there has been a massive decline, about 25 percent less coffee being consumed due to gastrointestinal distress. You know, that thing that happens in the stall on the right. I don't predict big success for the Folgers guys in this. I grew up

49

in a time and a place where if you asked at the local diner for decaf they looked at you like you were a Communist. Can you imagine the looks you would get if you ordered your coffee "simply smooth?" You would probably be tarred and feathered and run out of town on a rail. *Or then again I could be wrong.*

I gave up smoking in the time when cars still had ashtrays.

So it was a while ago and my memory may not be as sharp anymore but I don't think I just tossed my butts out the window. I know I spent some time every once in a while emptying the ashtray so I must have used it.

But nowadays smokers think nothing of tossing their butts out of car windows and it makes me crazy. In fact now that smoking is being banned everywhere the number of butts you see everywhere is becoming more than a nuisance. It's unhealthy too.

First off are those tossed butts from cars. It's just flat out wrong. If I tossed a soda can or bottle out that would be littering. Smokers think its ok that they toss out something that burns at about 1,000 degrees and could possibly set the world on fire.

I drive a low to the ground convertible. I have an intense nightmare where the discarded butt of some insensitive creep in front of me winds up in my car, sets the seats ablaze and I expire in a fiery crash. I have such pleasant nightmares.

Then there are those mounds of butts outside of anyplace that bans smoking inside. The real problem is twofold. First of all, contrary to popular belief, those butts are made of plastic, not cotton and they do not decompose. They will be on the ground longer then the pyramids.

Secondly, they are filters. They trap poisons that smokers would otherwise suck into their lungs. Poisons like acetone, ammonia, arsenic, benzene, cyanide, DDT, formaldehyde, lead and methyl isocyanate. If that last one doesn't sound familiar its accidental release killed 2000

51

people in Bhopal, India in 1984. If a truck tipped over carrying these chemicals, the guys in the HazMat suits would be cleaning it up.

Yet we turn a blind eye to smokers who spread these deathly concentrated poisons in our path everyday. So what's the solution? Pocket ashtrays. A quick Google search shows a bunch of different types ranging from fireproof pouches to tough cases made of abs non-flammable plastic in a variety of attractive colors. It even comes with a belt buckle clip. The price point on most of these disposal systems for butts is around a buck.

So here's my plan. Make them part of the cigarette purchase. Fasten them directly to the packs and pass the cost along to the smokers. Then make it a crime to smoke without one. And make the homeless guys in Public Square the enforcement officers. Eventually we could make smoking well, a pain in the butt. *Or then again I could be wrong.*

I had trouble sleeping again last night.

L ately that hasn't been the case. I was sick for a while
    this past month so I slept pretty soundly although
it was a medicated sleep.

I really didn't mind so much last night. Oh, I am
paying for it today. My eyes are burning from lack of
sleep and I am sure my brain is not up to par.

But last night was one of those nights where the
wind in the trees was creating a song for me that was
almost worth losing sleep for. Early in the morning when
the infernal traffic dies down on the road near my
bedroom, I can hear all sorts of things if I care to listen.
The geese down on the pond across the road make a
sound like people talking. Sometimes they take wing, fly
over the house and then recede, honking into
the distance.

I have a set of heavy duty wind chimes that we got
in Maine. When they get enough wind they gong like a
buoy in the ocean. The trees outside my window are still
loaded with leaves and the wind sifting through them and
the branches scraping against each other make a
soothing counterpoint.

An occasional burst of wind will find its way into
the room, ruffling the curtains and feeling cool and fresh
on my face. It's nights like these I wish I could somehow
sleep outdoors, and let the wind wash over me. Of course
our resident bear might persuade me otherwise. *Or then
again I could be wrong.*

I hate it when people throw cig butts out the window.

In general I think littering should be a bigger crime than it is. It's rude, vile and disgusting. But in case of the butts, it's dangerous too.

Why is it ok to flick a lit cigarette out of a car window? What are the ashtrays for, anyway? I can't tell you how many times I have ridden behind someone in my little roller skate MG with the top down and prayed that the tossed butt wouldn't land in my car.

I haven't smoked for a long, long time. So long that I can't really tell you if I used to chuck the tail ends of my smoke out the window. I do know most of what I was smoking *when I was smoking* wouldn't ever have been thrown away. *Heh.*

I now chew gum and my wife gets livid with me when I spit it out the window. I fail to see where that's as bad as the butts. The gum won't catch anything on fire. It will disintegrate with time unlike the filters on the butts which will probably be around for a millennium or two. And the worst that might happen is you might get my wad on your shoe.

Why does it piss me off so much when someone tosses a butt out? Why do I want to grab a lit cigarette and toss it in their window? I think I need therapy. *But then again I could be wrong.*

One of my pet peeves is people who ask, "Who's calling?" when they answer the phone for someone.

I feel like saying, "Whose business is it?" But I don't. Why do they need to know that? If I give the wrong name will I be put on permanent hold?

I bet most of the time the person answering doesn't even pass the name along. Why do I say that? Because when I am in particularly playful mood I will give an obviously fake name. I like to use Mcganahan Skijellyfetti. It's the name the Grateful Dead used for some of their publishing. The phone person invariably ask me to spell it and I will spell it with as many consonants as I possibly can.

Then when I am put through the other person will never even comment on my stupid ruse. I guess I have too much time on my hands.

I have been driving the speed limit now for almost a year.

I am the only person in the United States who does this and let me tell you it's a lonely life on the road. Here are the advantages of driving the posted limits on our nation's highways. I see stuff. Some of my daily drive is on country roads. I see nature's beauty in all its glory and I can really examine it. Last night there must have been 100 Canadian geese on a small pond that I inspected on my slow drive home. I have seen fox and mink recently along with a stately heron standing on one leg.

I also see things for sale. Lately loads of big SUVs parked by the side of the road, owners no doubt hoping to dump the gas guzzlers.

Which brings me to my next advantage. I really save gas at slower speeds. In this day of nearly $3 a gallon gas you would think that would be some incentive. Judging by the rest of the country whizzing by me, no.

Another positive is state of mind. Instead of arriving at my destination breathing like a track star and with hands sweaty and in pain from a death grip on the steering wheel I arrive relaxed.

This slower speed travel also lends itself to thinking. I do some of my best cogitating and reflection time at 55 mph on the interstate when the left hand lane screams by at 75 mph or more.

At legal speed limits I see police enforcement vehicles and don't hit the brakes and my heart rate stays normal. The big advantage is risk reduction. My slow speed allows me to see and to anticipate the possibility that the traffic ahead of me will turn into twisted piles of metal, flesh and blood.

There are some disadvantages to slow poke travel. I have to leave earlier for my appointments. Oh well. The rest of the traveling world seems pissed off at me. They ride my bumper, beep the horns and throw me colorful gestures. I am getting to the point where I don't take it personally. I pity them instead because they know not the peace of slow motion motoring.

Try as I might I can't come up with anything else negative. I do spend a little more time in the car than I used to. But it gives me more time to listen to my favorite radio station. And how can that be a bad thing? *But then again I could be wrong.*

I have lived in Vermont, New Hampshire and Maine among other places.

I used to hunt deer and I have spent countless hours in the woods during my life. I have seen thousands of deer, many foxes, a wolf or two, and even one very memorable time a bull moose in full rut charging our Jeep.

I have heard bear in the woods. They sometimes make a peculiar "hooting" sound when they communicate with one another at a distance. That noise always raises the hair on the back on my neck and returns me to shelter real fast. I never saw one up close. Or even at a distance.

Last week our indestructible squirrel-proof bird feeder bit the dust. I love feeding the birds. I will even put a corn cob or two out for the squirrels cause I think they are funny to watch. This bird feeder is truly a work or art. It's smooth metal with sloping sides and has foiled nearly every attempt by the grey rodents to get at its contents for almost 10 years. It's bolted to the tree with strong hardware. Friday morning it was on the ground. *Hmm*...I thought we have super squirrel. Put it back up. On the ground again on Saturday a.m. Put it up again. Sunday, same result. Of course you know it wasn't a squirrel.

We also have two plastic feeders suction cupped to our kitchen window. There really is nothing like having a cup of coffee and seeing chickadees, nuthatches, finches and the occasional titmouse so close to you that you can count feathers. Sunday night about 8 p.m. when it was just getting dark (curse you Daylight Savings Time) I heard a small voice from the kitchen as I watched TV in the living room. "Jim," my wife said very softly.

"He's here!" I ran to the kitchen and looked out the window at a BIG black bear!

It was looking in the window (about 6 feet off the ground) and didn't seem at all bothered by our presence. Certainly not as bothered as I was by his! He stretched out his neck and popped one plastic feeder off the window with his rather large jaws. Bear in mind (no pun intended) his face and ours were about two feet apart, separated by a sheet of glass! Carried it over to the center of our back yard, sat back and opened that sucker up like a Pez dispenser and poured the seeds down his throat. Stood up, took a dump (big!) and sauntered over and got the other feeder.

By this time I was snapping pictures as fast as the flash would recycle. My wife thought it would enrage the beast but he couldn't have cared less. He snuffed around our yard for a while even climbed a tree, to look around I guess, and then left.

Our 911 call got us a nice police officer about half an hour after "Yogi" left. We walked around but he was gone. The pictures are a big disappointment. The flash lit up the window great, but caused too much glare to really see him clear. But if you look close, you can see his bear face. Just another day, on the mountain.

I have never really had a run in with the police.

I have had my share of what the troopers call moving violations. On one memorable occasion I was stopped for speeding on the interstate in town whose name ends in "-kill" in another state. Even though I was being passed by someone when the trooper turned on his flashing lights. I stopped and when the man with the hat approached I asked in what I thought was a calm voice about it. He replied something like there was only me. I called the trooper a bad word followed by the word liar. I am still not sure why he didn't arrest me, or at least shoot me.

But I can't hold a candle to the guy they found walking around Luzerne, Pennsylvania a while ago. About midnight in the night in question, this fellow was walking with what officers said was unsteady balance. And when they asked him for identification they detected a strong odor of alcohol. It was at this point he began to growl like a dog and tried biting the officers.

Like I say. I can't even begin to imagine the thought process involved here. The police are bothering me. I am drunk as a skunk. How about I pretend I am Rin Tin Tin.

The guy in question clocked in at 0.30 percent. The legal limit for driving in Pennsylvania is 0.08. I don't know what it is for walking or growling. By the way if you're curious our man turned Fido must have had at least 18 beers to get that high a reading. Oh and he is in the jail house on $5,000 bail. That's $277 per beer. *Or then again I could be wrong.*

***I have written before about people
talking on cell phones in public places.***

J ust to refresh your memory I am not in favor of it. I
find it unspeakably rude and really unnecessary. But
the other day really took the cake.

I was heading towards the entrance of the Barnes
& Noble in Wilkes-Barre, Pennsylvania and I noticed a
man pacing the sidewalk with the ubiquitous cell phone
to his ear. As I came closer I became aware that he was
displeased with the party on the other end of his call. I
quickly picked up on this because every third word out of
his mouth was the f-word. And not quietly either. As a
matter of fact I started to hear the word that rhymes with
truck when I was still in the parking lot.

I looked around. A big minivan (doesn't that
sound like an oxymoron?) was parked with the doors
open and several people were helping Grandma get out
probably to shop for a Bible. This guy was crossing their
path shouting obscenities into the phone like he was a
longshoreman down at the docks. I stood there with my
mouth open in utter shock and dismay.

Now I am no stranger to expletives. But I am
careful to be aware of my surroundings when I let loose
and I find I am being more thoughtful about things like
volume and echo then before.

So anyway this guy is using the f-word as a verb,
an adjective, a pronoun and a few other grammatical
miracles while Grandma and family are within earshot.
Heck, the entire shopping mall was within earshot. And
I couldn't help but think, what gives him this right?

So I stopped and stared at him. Not threatening.
I don't do confrontation well. But like I was seeing a
traffic accident or maybe an animal with two heads. That

sort of look. I looked at him, caught his eye and looked over at Grandma, blue hair and all. I looked back at him and he didn't care.

I wish I could say I grabbed his phone and pistol whipped him with it. I wish I could say I got in his face and put some manners on him. I wish I could, but I didn't. I held the door for Grandma and left him on the sidewalk with his gutter mouth and his anger.

I am a deep believer in karma. I am sincerely believing that this oaf will come back in his next life clutching a turd to his ear instead of a cell phone and be walking barefoot thru razor blades in a puddle of battery acid. *But then again I could be wrong.*

I have written here a few times about the joys of being a homeowner in Northeast Pennsylvania.

B ut nothing compares with the fun and excitement that I have when I clear the leaves every year. I have regaled you with my leafy adventures more than once and it may be that I have crossed the line from telling a story to an obsession. But be that as it may, it needs one more brush of the keyboard before I put the leaves to bed for the year.

Although it was a clear day it was as cold as a witch's mammary gland in a brass bra. Even with gloved hands and two layers of clothing I could feel winter's impending arrival clearly. But the work went well enough. I was just about finished when the lawn tractor got stuck again.

For those of you keeping score this makes the third time in as many years that this has happened. The previous years were in entirely different spots on the property. I was totally unprepared for this place to be wet and muddy but the trusty lawn tractor went for it like Dale Earnhardt, Jr. for the checkered flag.

I am now of the opinion that my Sears Craftsmen 42 inch 12 horsepower with rear baggers must have been a pig in a former life. It seems to sense mud and wallows in it with obscene pleasure.

The infernal beast was stuck sideways on a steep hill. Job one was to get the nose pointing uphill. This involved actually picking the front end up (where the engine lives) and placing it delicately back down several times while my feet did ballet-like maneuvers in the mud. Having it oriented in the right direction I placed old roof shingles under the rear wheels for traction. Some of those may be found someday as they flew out from under the wheels like excrement out of a goose and disappeared into the stratosphere.

So the only solution was to get behind and push. The Sears folks engineered an interlock on the seat of the mower. Unless your keester is in the seat, it just won't run. I outfoxed their best designs and found that by piling 20 bricks on the seat the thing would run on its own. You can pretty much guess the rest here. When I finally got enough mud on me, the darn thing started to move. And all at once took off. I, of course, fell nose first in the mud and the blood. A short footrace later, I caught up with the tractor before it hit a tree. I hit the tree instead and then cushioned the tractors impact with my own body which knocked the wind out of me and the bricks off the seat halting the mud- loving mower. Only several bricks hit my feet, so I was fine.

It's over for the year now. And in a short time, I may actually be able to move again without little spasms of pain everywhere. *Or then again I could be wrong.*

I know more about the guy, sitting across from me at lunch the other day, then I want to.

It happens more and more often lately. I will be having a pleasant lunch with a business associate or maybe even a friend. The restaurant is busy with a lunch time crowd but we can still chat and make ourselves understood.

Then it happens. The annoying cell phone ring from the next table. Now I carry a cell phone every waking moment. I never know when an urgent need for my expertise (Jim, the toilet at the studio is overflowing) will be called upon. But I keep mine on vibrate. So if I choose to ignore it, no one else knows.

But everyone else has some tune. The ones that really annoy me are the half-assed ring tones that are supposed to sound like popular songs. And why do they have to be so LOUD! A cell phone is usually on your person, right? So why have the gosh darn thing turned up to concert level decibels?

But that's just the beginning. The guy's phone begins to blast out "Crazy Frog" at ear-bleeding volume. He unclips it and stares at the screen to see who is calling. So let's tally up what's going on. He has decided to be rude to his luncheon companion by pulling out the phone. He is being inconsiderate to the rest of the world by assaulting our ears with the ring tone. And he is being rude to whoever is trying to call him because he is not answering until he decides they are important enough for him to talk to at that time.

He makes his choice. Disses his lunch buddy and takes the call. And proceeds to have the most inane conversation ever at the top of his lungs. "HELLO GEORGE! WHAT? OH NOTHING. JUST SAT

DOWN TO EAT! YEAH? HAR HAR HAR! OH YOUR KIDDING! HOLY GOD! HAR HAR!" and then this guy starts to talk about his previous night's date in not so subtle terms.

Now I am trying to continue my chat with my lunch companion but it's not possible. I am trying not to listen to the conversation between this moron in the restaurant and George but it's like trying not to think of the colors blue and white in State College.

Is there a device that you can point at cell phones and make them blow up? Invent one and you will be rich beyond your wildest dreams.

I love ice cream.

G ive me a cone or a dish of the frosty sweet concoction and I will eat it. Like sex, I don't think there is such a thing as bad ice cream. Some is better than others but as the saying goes, it's all good.

I live not too far from Hillside Dairy where quite possibly the best ice cream in the Free World and maybe even the universe is made. You can take your Ben and Jerry's and your Häagen-Dazs and stack them up against some Whitehouse cherry at Hillside and I know who will win, spoons down.

And speaking of Whitehouse and ice cream (and this my friends is what is known as a segue) how about the time the leader of the Free World came to our neck of the woods and had himself a cone? You had to have heard about it. George W. was in the area trying to convince us that Don Sherwood was or is a good guy and deserving of re-election to whatever cushy job he has in our nation's capital. After heaping praise on Don, the president hopped in the big limo and had his secret service agents drive him to Manning's Ice Cream in Scranton for a dip.

I am looking at one of the photos as I write this. Don Sherwood is standing next to George holding his dish of ice cream and grinning like a ninny. The President of the United States of America is holding his cone carefully well away from his suit and has a very odd look on his face. I think upon careful study that George looks like he would rather not be holding the cone or else maybe not standing next to the grinning ninny Don. I know it's a lot to read into a picture but I call'em as I see'em. The other impression that I get is that the last thing on either of these two men's minds is the ice cream.

The cone and dish are just props for the photo op and I am willing to bet that neither one of them actually ate or enjoyed the sweet treat.

And that my friend is the ultimate tragedy of our political system. Power and politics have overshadowed the simple pleasure of ice cream and in my book that's just a shame. *Or then again I could be wrong.*

I love letters to the editor in the newspapers.

I t reveals tons about the true way many people here in northeastern Pennsylvania view life, the world and the way things should be. The letters that I really enjoy are the ones that end with the words, "something should be done." Pigeon poop? Something should be done. Casino gambling coming to our area? Something should be done. Cops driving too fast? Something should be…wait a minute. Cops driving too fast?

Yes, this was an actual letter to the editor in the *Times Leader* the other day. A guy we will call Casey because that is his name, wrote in and said, "The police in our area break the speed limit constantly." Casey who is from Shavertown continued, "I have seen so many cops in Nanticoke, Swoyersville, Dallas, Shavertown and Trucksville going well over twice the legal limit." Casey goes on to say "Police on the Cross Valley fly past everyone in the passing lane doing 80-100 miles an hour." Casey ended his letter with "something needs to be done," a permissible variance on the "something should be done" theme.

Casey is, of course, deranged. But let's for a moment let Casey's idea seem like a good one. Let's make the cops drive the speed limit while they are on the way to a bank robbery or to a homicide. In fact, let's put speed governors on the cruisers to prevent them from going over 55 mph ever. Why stop there? Those fire trucks and ambulances are all speed demons too. Why should we let someone suffering a heart attack get to the E.R. any quicker than Casey gets to the store to buy a quart of milk? *Hmmm?* I am just getting started here.

In Casey's world there are many instances where people of authority abuse that same authority and it probably makes him mad as hell. I hesitate to put words in Casey's mouth but I am sure our friend from Shavertown would agree here. Why should those cruisers and fire trucks and ambulances have those loud sirens? If they are going to the speed limit they won't need the noisemakers will they? And let's not get started about those flashing lights. They could cause a seizure. Muzzle the noisemakers! Unplug the bubble lights! Something should be done!

Oh, and why do the cops need to carry those big guns strapped to their sides? What possible reason can you think of for a cop to need a weapon when he's directing traffic at a high school football game? What could possibly happen at a school for heaven's sake? In Casey's world the slow unarmed cops and the silent fire trucks and ambulances work just fine. *And then again I could be wrong.*

I make a lot of phone calls in the course of my business days.

R eturning calls is something that I have come to dread and it has nothing to do with the reluctance to do my job. Instead it is the roadblocks that get placed in front of you when you are just trying to talk on the phone to somebody.

First on my list of things that make you want to throw the phone in the trash can are cell phones. Cell phones, when they work are a boon to modern communication. Where before you often couldn't reach someone because they were out of the office or away from their desk now they are on an electronic leash that you can pull on almost anytime.

The problems occur when the cell service sucks, which it often does. How many times can you laugh over the phrase, "Can you hear me now?" before you want to find the cell phone tower and chop it down? Then when the call gets cut off, you are left with the option of trying to get reconnected, which can take some time and wear out your patience even more, or risk leaving the impression that you just hung up on the other party. Neither one is an attractive option.

Beyond cell phone madness are the gatekeepers at the front desk. Some receptionists must have strict instructions not to let anyone talk to their boss. The first line of defense is the question, "Whom may I say is calling?" Right away I feel defensive. What if I am not important enough to be put through? Then comes the killer for me. "What is this regarding?" I am often tempted to say something really silly, like this call is about his house being on fire, or the pictures the

71

detective took of his wife having an affair are in, can he make time to review them, but I don't.

The next roadblock is of course the answering machine. Why is it that some folks think that the outgoing message on the answering device has to be cute or funny? I am not amused by celebrity imitations poorly done inviting me to leave my message. And I don't need to hear your favorite song before you finally let me record. By the way the long-winded explanation of how and when to do my thing could go as well. I think we all know how the things work by now. Don't we?

But the worst impediment to getting the person to the phone is when the three-year-old answers. No matter what you say you are not going to get mom or dad on the phone without a battle. Mostly what happens is the phone gets set down after a few incomprehensible words are exchanged and you are left wondering if you will ever hear from an adult again. And kids on the answering machine? Shoot me now. *Or then again I could be wrong.*

I saw regular gas for $2.57 the other day.

The price of gas has risen 20 cents in the last month. About a dime overnight at one station I drive by. I saw a station at $2.49 over the weekend. You couldn't really see the pumps. It was overrun with people trying to fill up at a few cents savings.

It's headed for $3 a gallon folks. Do the math with me. I have three cars: 16 gallons in one, 14 in another and 10 in my little MG. If I fill them each up once a week, not too far fetched a scenario, it'll take $126 to drive away from the pumps at $3 a gallon.

With gas becoming this expensive a couple of things are gonna start happening. Northeast Pennsylvania has always been a target for creeps from New York and Philadelphia to scurry in to town and knock over our convenience stores. Now gas stations will be prime candidates for robbers.

Drive-offs, as the gas stations call people who steal gas by pumping and leaving, will become commonplace. It will end in extreme measures like armed guards at the pumps, mark my words.

Those big tanker trailers hold 12 thousand gallons of the juice as Mel Gibson called it in *Mad Max*, At $3, that's $36,000 rolling around waiting for someone with a notion and not much sense to run off with. So if they aren't already you can bet the tanker truck drivers will be packing heat. How long before they install tail-gunners? It's all gonna end in tears I fear.

I should have suspected something
was amiss when I saw the sign.

O r rather didn't see the sign. It was covered in a blue tarp. We actually drove by the joint because it was late at night and it was after a nine hour drive.

Let me back up here. Thanksgiving week we were out of town visiting relatives. My cost-conscious sister booked a hotel for us. Now I am the first guy to want to save a buck or two, but there are limits. I kinda knew there was a problem when I couldn't get the number of the hotel from directory assistance. The problem was that this dog kennel claiming to be a hotel had changed names and owners five times in as many years. Hence the covered sign.

The check-in process brought little comfort. The TV in the waiting area was at jet-landing-on-the-air-craft-carrier volume. It was so loud I could feel my eardrums compressing. And the lobby was hot. Too hot for comfort. I mean Africa hot.

Now the night clerk was a big man. I am the last to point fingers at anyone with a weight problem. But this guy was way beyond a weight problem. He was a weight catastrophe. And the heat wasn't helping him out either. Let's just say he wasn't smelling shower fresh and we will leave it at that. So here I am hot, sweaty, tired and shouting at a man who could kill me. A Norman Rockwell painting it was not. The sign on the check-in desk said something about mold. I was too tired to care. Did I mention we were at the end of 12 hour drive? *Um hmmm.*

Crawled to our room. There were a grand total of four lights in the room. The entry light didn't work. As soon as I turned on the one by the TV it flashed bright and never went on again. The circuit breaker must have blown because the TV didn't work either.

So now we have two lights and no power plug that works to plug in my cell phone or computer. I have to check my email. Wait they don't have WiFi so I will have to connect up to the phone with a modem. Usually not a problem but the phone has no instruction plate on it. A quick call to the front desk got this response, "Follow the instructions on your phone."

"I have none," I cried.

"Well, I don't either. Sorry." Barnum and Bailey's loss hung up on me.

Now why would we stay? Did I mention we had just driven 24 hours? And it was Thanksgiving eve? The fact that the bathroom had paint all over the floor began to make it all add up. They were renovating. We were in a hotel construction zone.

A restless night later I rise early to investigate the complimentary breakfast. It was in the atrium. Yes, this was a huge room. Had a big, sit-down area by the indoor pool. Ah yes, the pool. Ever see *National Lampoon's Vacation*? The Grizwolds arrive at the campground and the kids are all excited about the swimming pool? Until they look in it and discover two feet of green slime with ducks swimming in it? Sort of like that.

I begin to notice two things. First, there is an odor. Couldn't quite put my finger on it. Second, it's 35 degrees in this atrium. The complimentary breakfast? Let's just say that it was no compliment. In fact, it was an insult.

Looking around I see what looks like police crime scene tape over half the doors. Being a curious guy I went to the front desk (the 500 pound desk clerk was off duty, thanks be to God) and asked. "Oh, those are the rooms we can't use because of the mold problem," the new desk clerk said cheerfully pointing to the sign I had glanced at last night.

We were supposed to stay three nights at this pleasure palace. As I was checking out, which was right after she pointed at the mold sign I said – and this was exactly what I said, "This is not your fault, I understand that but this is the worst excuse for a hotel I have ever seen. It smells, the lights don't work and I wouldn't let my dog stay here. You shouldn't even be open never mind charging people to stay here. I'll let the owners know."

She actually said, "Have a nice day." Now that's customer service. *Or then again I could be wrong.*

I sit upright at the table and don't chew with my mouth open.

W hy would a restaurant want to make me feel like I was a second class citizen? A while ago one of the restaurants in my area changed owners and pretty much everything else. What it lost in the transition was my patronage.

My long suffering wife and I have a rotation of places that we visit. We don't really eat out that much so we like variety and when we like a place we will put it into our list. Depending on the mood, the timing and our finances we will visit The Dough Company, Pickett's Charge, Thyme at the Woodlands, Isabella, Tony Stella's Good-Fellos, Twigs in Tunkhannock, and any number of chains like the Olive Garden and Outback.

Some of those places mentioned are what you would consider fancy. They have real silverware and linen tablecloths and good wine lists. I am not intimidated by any of this. I can be relied upon not to break wind at the table or spit on the floor. I think I am a reasonably classy guy and I can appreciate the finer things in life.

So why when we visited this place that has changed owners, menu and attitude were we treated like scum? I would have classified this joint as fancy until they proved to me that they are really a hot dog stand. First of all a 20 minute wait to be seated in an empty restaurant is just plain rude. No apology. No explanation. I should have known then what I was in for.

Then when seated in the empty room they sat us next to the serving station. So all during the meal in the EMPTY restaurant we were treated to the busboys and wait staff gossiping three feet from our table. When they weren't talking they were listening to our conversation. Nice.

The food was ok. For the price range it was just ok. The entrees were presented like it was a four star deal and the prices reflect that but it's a joint in northeastern Pennsylvania with a view of a busy highway...not Fifth Avenue.

Service was slow and indifferent to downright rude. Asking for more water brought no response.

"More water, please?" Nope.

"Do you have any water here?" Just indifference.

"Can I pay for water? If I was on fire would you pee on me?"

Possibly we weren't the type of clientele they were looking for. My money, however spends just as well elsewhere. As for the fancy hot dog stand? I have had better service and food at the Rising Ranch Wagon. We have never returned. I am certain they don't miss us. *But then again I could be wrong.*

I suffer from "Where's a cop now?" disease.

M aybe you are familiar with the syndrome. The symptoms flare up when I see some stupid behavior on the highways and byways of northeast Pennsylvania go unpunished.

Maybe it's just me. But I know when I commit even the slightest infraction that justice is swift and sure. Let me roll through a stop sign at three in the morning when there is no other vehicle on the road for hundreds of miles and the long arm of the law will tap me on the shoulder and hand me a moving violation.

But I witness on a daily basis such amazing flaunting of traffic laws that I am literally dumfounded. At first I wrote speechless but I am definitely not speechless. And mostly what you hear me shout is, "Where's a cop now?"

Here's a case in point. I was sitting at a red light the other day when I saw a Jeep pull into a bank parking lot on my right. It caught my attention because the Jeep was moving at a high rate of speed and nearly hit the curb. I have driven many jeeps and can tell you from experience that they have a high center of gravity and tend to tip over in such conditions.

So I watched the vehicles progress with some interest hoping not to see it on its side in the near future. The Jeep raced through the parking lot, out the other side and in the process avoided waiting for the traffic light which I was stuck at. Where's a cop now, I thought.

And that's just one example of the many, many scofflaws I see on a daily basis. Never mind the speeders that blow past me like I am tied to a post. Don't worry about the idiots who weave through lanes on the interstate like they are on a slalom course from hell. And just forget about the person who passed me on the right hand shoulder the other day, throwing rocks, beer cans and who knows what else 50 feet in the air in an effort to get ahead of me at all costs. Let those guys go.

But if you see me driving with a tail light out, be sure to throw the book at me. Maybe all cars should be equipped with a video recorder in the grill. It would run constantly and be automatically downloaded at the touch of a button to the police. They could review the tapes and….nah. What am I thinking? They don't have time to do any such thing. They are way to busy ignoring the guys who pull around red lights through bank parking lots. *Or then again I could be wrong.*

I think that our experience
with birthdays goes in cycles.

W hen we are young we can't wait for the day with the promise of presents and cake. In our middle age we begin to dread the passing of another year and the attendant decline it signifies. But now that I am on the side where there are less birthdays left than I have already celebrated I am beginning to appreciate them all over again.

I have a friend who found a way to celebrate his birthday twice. He was delighted recently that his math was wrong. He was pretty sure going into his birthday celebration that he was a year older than he actually was. His delight was very great when he discovered he had cheated the calendar by 365 days. So now he has a whole year to enjoy all over again. Or something like that.

The long suffering wife had a birthday lately. She has never said so but I don't think she enjoys being another year older. While she takes it all in her usual good natured way she is not too interested in me baking a cake and doing the candle thing.

But the celebration of a loved one's birthday doesn't have to be the ritual that involves the singing of the dreaded song and the huffing and puffing over a cake in flames. I know quite a few people who take their birthdays off from work. I have a relative who manages somehow to get the entire week surrounding his birthday off.

But I don't know many guys who take their wife's birthday off. But having done just that recently I am going to make a habit of it from now on. I lose vacation days every year because I am too busy to take all that I am owed. "Busy is as busy does," as Forrest Gump would say and I am going to make a diligent effort this year to come out even.

One part of that effort was spending the day off with the long suffering wife. We truly did nothing special. Nothing that we wouldn't have done on a typical Saturday. A little ride and a peek or two at the antique stores on the way. A lunch in a favorite restaurant. A day with no particular agenda and that was just fine.

I guess as the number of birthdays you have left in your life decreases the important thing is not so much the presents and the cake, but the time spent in the company of those we love. This is in no way saying that when my next birthday arrives that cake and presents will go unappreciated. If there is something that tastes as good as birthday cake and ice cream, I have yet to discover it. *Or then again I could be wrong.*

I took a job quite a few years back at a radio station that will remain nameless for the purpose of this narrative.

I t was a station that was in probably the oldest facility I have ever worked at and the joint had only two bathrooms. The ladies' room was near the lobby and the men's room was all the way in the back, but near the sales offices.

You know there are lots of things they don't tell you when you start a job at any office but what I didn't know was the sink in the men's room was routinely used to fill the coffee pot for the sales team, many of which has no business being in the men's room. If you get my drift.

The protocol which I was not privy to (pun intended) was for female coffee makers to knock on the men's room door before entering. I was blissfully unaware of this while doing my business at the urinal when I heard a knock at the door. Not thinking and done but not buttoned up I turned towards the door and showed my shortcomings to a very flustered sales girl.

My next stop was the general manger's office where I opened the conversation with, "I just exposed my self to a sales girl. Am I fired?" We all had a good laugh.

But the other day was not nearly as funny. I was done with my workout and stumbling to the locker room. Went in and passed by the couple in the sink area on my way to the shower. Wait a minute. A couple in the men's locker room. Man and woman. And in an embrace. That seemed, well, wrong.

I walked back over to confirm what I saw and was greeted with cold stares. As though I was intruding. I really didn't know what to say so I said nothing. It's worth noting here that that the guy part of this little incident was the same one who unplugged my treadmill while I was going full tilt and was to put it mildly, less than apologetic. So we already sort of knew each other.

I went back to the shower area and sat down to consider my options. I could wait. I could continue my routine. I could suggest to them that they get a room. In the end they solved the problem for me by leaving. Maybe they went in the ladies' room. Some countries have unisex bathrooms. I never want to go there. *Or then again I could be wrong.*

I try to present a lighthearted demeanor to the world.

A lthough sometimes I don't really feel upbeat I am in the words of Billy Joel, "Quick with a joke and to light up your smoke." I have found that a little levity greases the wheels of social interaction. Sometimes I do carry it a bit too far.

One of my favorite pranks used to be standing at a door and waiting for someone to open it. I would slap the door hard and then grab my head as though they had slammed my noggin. Hilarious.

The old tire trick is a good one too. When someone drives away you jump and down and point at the back tires. When they slow and roll down the window you tell them in a loud voice, "Your back wheels are turning." It's kind of surprising how many people will stop and get out to look. I am just a barrel of laughs.

But my career as a jokester blew up in my face the other day. Sort of. The other day a small group of us had lunch together to send off a co-worker who had taken a job in another city. It was a great lunch with loads of paint thinner consumed along with much good humor.

As we returned to the car I wrapped my hand around the door post to help me climb in the back seat of the minivan. The guest of honor was riding shotgun and without knowing my hand was in the way slammed the door.

First of all let me say that if you have never had your hand slammed in a car door, I would not recommend it. The pain is beyond any sort of pain I have felt before and I paid alimony for a long time. I yelled out, "Open the door!" over and over again.

The guys in the front seat, of course thought Jim the Jester was making a joke. So it took a little while for them to see that I was this time, serious. In a detached sort of way I was watching the guy in the front seat as he realized I was in real trouble and then it was sort of amusing to see him scramble to find the door handle. Sort of amusing.

My hand swelled up to the size of ballpark franks and took on all the colors of a sunrise, but it doesn't seem to be broken. So maybe I should lay off the jokes for a while, what do you think? But the rear tire trick is so good. *Or then again I could be wrong.*

I type a lot.

B ut I never learned to type like a pro. I took the class in high school. But the teacher was such an anal retentive "bee-acth" that I guess it soured me on learning the right way ever again.

But I can type really fast the two finger way. And now with the word processor and spell-check and grammer check and truth check you barely need to type anything anyway. The computer does almost all of it for you. But I still need to look at the keyboard to see what I am typing.

That's why I was kinda amazed to see the newest thing for the computer geek in your life. A keyboard with nothing printed on the keys. One hundred four blank keys. Perfect for composing blank verse. Sorry I couldn't resist. It's on the web at *daskeyboard.com* for $80.

It made me think about other things we use in daily life that would be interesting without numbers. How about phones with no numbers on the keypad. I mean you know where they are, right? Think of all the ink we could save. TV remote controls with no channel numbers. A truly random viewing experience. Microwave touch pads without numbers. An adventure in over and under done taste. Elevators with no numbers for floors. Live a little. Take a different floor every time till you hit the right one. Ban house numbers. Pay unexpected visits to total strangers trying to find the right place. ATMs with blank keypads. Think of all the money you'd save by not being able to enter the correct pin code! *Or maybe I could be wrong.*

I used to drive fast.

Really fast. At 17-years-old I was clocked in my parents' station wagon (a Vista Cruiser!) at 120 mph in a four wheel brakes locked skid. The cop who did the clocking said, and this is exactly what he said, "They won't none believe this at the courthouse. Go on. Git outta here. And when you kill yerself don't take no one with ya."

When I was 21, I moved to Jacksonville, North Carolina to work at a real bad radio station. That's a whole rant right there. If you want to live in a real redneck town Jacksonville will do just fine. It's the home of the "World's Largest Amphibian Marine Base." I should have know it was gonna be trouble when that was printed on the letterhead of the radio station's correspondence with me.

On my first trip into work, at 6 a.m. on Sunday morning (late as usual) I went 65 mph in a 25 mph school zone. It was Sunday morning at 6 a.m. for crying out loud! The law in North Carolina is if you go 25 miles past the speed limit you are charged with intent to commit homicide with a motor vehicle.

This time the cop did not say, "Git." They put me in jail cell for a day. And took away my license for six months. I rode my bike to work every day. It rains in North Carolina. A lot. I arrived at work with a wet dog smell every day for six months until I got my license back.

Then they canned me....I used to drive fast. I traveled between here (northeastern Pennsylvania) and Portsmouth, New Hampshire on a regular basis for a while. It's a six hour trip, at posted speed limits. I could do it in less than five hours but you wouldn't want to ride with me. It was tailgating, flashing brights, horn blowing at slowpokes, left lane no slower than 85 mph, all the way. *Whee!*

I used to drive fast. I had moving violations in four states at the same time once. I got three of them the same day! I used to drive fast. But now I drive slow. Not real slow, but I do follow the posted speed limits.

And that's where the rant comes in. If you follow the speed limits on secondary roads in northeastern Pennsylvania you are considered an idiot by the people behind you.

How do I know this? Because when they pass me at the first possible opportunity they yell, "Get outta the way you f&*#ing idiot.!"

My response to the tailgating, horn blowing, finger giving, brights flashing, folks behind me? I go 5 mph BELOW the speed limit. And if they keep it up I drive even slower.

I have become an old fart. This drives my wife nuts. But I really don't do it to make her crazy. I just don't want any more tickets, and I don't enjoy driving fast on roads where deer and children, with the brains of deer, run out in front of you like they dropped from the sky.

When at all possible I will pull off and let everyone by me. But only if it's safe to do it and if you haven't given me the finger. So if you are trapped behind this old fart don't drive aggressively behind me...I will only hold you up even more.

I was on a road trip the other day – a long one – about six hours in a car with a couple of other radio guys.

I got to thinking about the reasons why I got in this business all those years ago. One reason will sound pretty silly. Or egomaniacal. Or something. When I was young in radio I used get the biggest thrill out of turning on the microphone switch and talking.

I could just picture that tiny switch controlling the thousands of watts going up into the huge towers, massive structures soaring into the sky. It was a big rush for me, and still is. Name another industry where one man alone (or woman, let's be PC here) can control such power with the flick of a wrist. Later on, of course I found the real source of power was the man or woman, behind the man or woman, with their hands on the switch, but that's another story.

Of course the real reason to get into radio was.....free records. Oh my gawd do they send radio stations free records. Piles of them. Stacks of them. And as part of my job I was supposed to TAKE THEM HOME AND LISTEN TO THEM!!! How much more wonderful could it be? I got free records to keep and they paid me (not much to be sure) to listen to them. And then I could play them on the air. And listen to them again! It was heaven.

Of course it couldn't last. The record became CDs and most of them were not real good. And there were SO many of them. You spent almost all your "free" time (ask my first wife) listening to crap. And felt guilty if you didn't.

And as for listening to them on the air...let me tell you a big secret. If you played the middle of almost any record on most stations to most announcers they wouldn't know who it was. They just hear the first and last 10 seconds. All the other time is spent talking on the request phone, setting up comedy bits, getting the weather and traffic reports and so on.

I went for an oil change the other day.

N ot my own but my long suffering wife's car. Like getting a haircut taking the car for it's 3,000 mile devotion is something all civilized people must do. I don't know about you but I feel terribly guilty when I look at the little sticker on the windshield and compare it with the odometer and notice that the car's time is due. My wife's car even yells at you with a yellow light that beseeches you to service engine soon when you start it up.

So in an effort to earn the ever more important brownie points I headed out to the fast oil change place. I have learned that some fast oil change places are better than others. The prices and the oil seem to be about the same but the level of competency in that pit can be wildly different.

On one memorable occasion I had my car's oil changed and immediately drove several hundred miles, most of them well over the posted speed limits. Near the end of my journey the check engine light came on so I pulled over. Now I am no mechanic but even I know you are supposed to replace the filler cap when you are done changing the oil. It had been left on top of the air filter and the engine was so hot from having all the new oil escape that the oil cap's impression had been burned into the air filter. That car took five quarts of convenience store oil before I saw any on the dip stick. Needless to say I crossed that particular oil change spot off my list.

Back to the oil change in question. I pulled up to the garage door and was happy to see that I would be next in when the car being serviced pulled out. Or so I thought. The attendant came out and I rolled down the window. "I'm sorry sir but you'll have to change lanes." I figured it out pretty quick. The guy in the other lane had arrived before me but now I would be getting in ahead of him as the car in the bay in front of me was done before the one in front of him. I obliged feeling somewhat noble about it.

Now here's the tricky part. When the car I traded places with was done the car in front of me was still not finished. I think they were replacing the engine. But now there was another car in the other lane. I saw the attendant come out and speak to the other driver who at first shook his head then dropped his vehicle in reverse and gunned his engine, squealing his tires in the process and pulling out way too fast in reverse. I was directed to the newly vacated spot and went in to get the job done.

The attendant apologized for playing what he called "musical cars" with me. He went on to say, "Some people, like that other guy get really mad but we have to take customers in the order they arrive."

I thought about it and said. "But we learned that in grade school. No cutting in line, right?"

The attendant just looked at me and smiled and said, "You don't work with the public much do you?"

As I pulled out I noticed that the same musical cars game was still being played. Whatever was wrong with that other car I was glad it wasn't my problem. *And about that I don't think I am wrong.*

I wish I understood how money works.

O h I know how to spend it, that's no problem. I can count how much I have and I can if I squint and rub my neck figure out how much change I should have coming. If I consult the little chart in my wallet I can even figure out the right amount to leave for a tip. But I am real confused on this whole tax thing.

A long time ago someone told me if you get a refund on your taxes that's a bad thing. His contention was that the best thing to have happen is to break even. If you pay taxes at tax time, you didn't have enough taken out of your paycheck over the past year. If you get a refund you had too much taken out and you made an interest free loan to the government.

Well I never followed his advice and I always end up getting a refund. It seems like a little present every year and I am ok with letting the government boys use my money. Lord knows they need it for wars and such. But then I get that tax refund. And what's the first thing I do with it? Pay my property taxes. Wait. What just happened here? I paid taxes out all year from my paycheck. I got my tax refund. I paid my taxes with it. I just don't get it. It seems like the money came in and went out like a magic trick. Did I miss something?

I seem to pay taxes to a bunch of places every year. The federal government. The great Commonwealth of Pennsylvania. My local taxes. Then on top of those I pay a right to work tax, my property taxes and later on this year my school taxes. I pay a tax on gasoline, wine and when we eat at a restaurant. What is going on here?

My tax return is real complicated. My very patient tax person told me a few years back that the first time she tried to do my forms she went home and cried. Now when I come in with my wheelbarrow full of receipts and stuff she just sighs. This year she called me up after she did my taxes and said that she had made a tiny mistake. When she figured out everything she forgot to add in the fact that I got a small refund from the local taxes.

So now if I understand this correctly I am taxed on the refund for my taxes and I have to pay the tax on that. As Daffy Duck once said to Bugs Bunny, "Shoot me now." *Or then again I could be wrong.*

I wonder sometimes what would happen if the
thin line between civilized behavior and no holds
barred, bull goose loonyness were to be crossed.

I t seems to me that the thing we call civilization is really just a layer of chrome plating over some really ugly bare metal and if you scrape that stuff off then our true nature – warts and all – would be revealed.

The other day someone said to me that I have become calmer lately and I guess that is true. At least within earshot of others I don't fly into spit-flying, eye-popping, uncontrolled rages as often as I used to. We practice day-to-day good manners. At least most of say please or thank you, hold doors open and wipe our mouths off when eating soup.

But what would have to happen before our true natures were revealed? A bunch of noisy kids in a restaurant might be a good test case. Ever sit near a table full of kids? Maybe six or seven little rug rats, aged one to six? A couple of adults with them who don't seem to notice the shrieking, food-tossing, tantrum-throwing chaos around them. They calmly eat their meals while we at the next table over have our nerves shattered by ear-piercing screams and ceaseless other annoyances.

On the outside I remain calm and wish I was elsewhere, but inside I want to grab those little brats by the legs and swing them against the wall till their brains splatter. You see what I mean? It's just below the surface. How many times, how much would it take to push me, Mr. Calm into a homicidal frenzy, leaving a blood-soaked path in my wake? A lot, I hope.

If you watch the cop shows on TV or read the local police blotter in the newspaper you often see it. Everyday people, usually fueled by booze or some other mind-altering substance engaged in the act of peeling off the chrome. The easy excuse is that the booze or drugs are doing the dirty work but I don't think that's the total answer. I think lurking just beneath that little layer of polish on all of us, underneath the shiny stuff there is the primordial urge to pull someone's head off and put it on a pike.

In many ways we have progressed but I bet the buttons that turn us back into cavemen in most cases aren't totally disconnected. Just ask the guy who is on trial for organizing September 11th. I know, he must be crazy, right? Maybe he just ran out of chrome polish. *But then again I could be wrong.*

I have never been in a real fist fight.

W hen I was in junior high school a kid wanted to beat me up and kept up a steady war of pushing and shoving and punching my arm in the hallways. Eventually the bully got to me by making fun of my then girlfriend so I agreed to meet him after school. It was the usual deal with all his buddies gathered around to egg him on and he landed the first punch, bloodying my nose. All I remember after that was picking him up off the ground and throwing him down until he didn't get up anymore. He never bothered me again. I tell you this because I came as close as I have in my adult life to throwing a punch the other day and it was over something so stupid I can't believe it.

The long suffering wife and I ventured to Wal-Mart. The mission: to buy me a new pair of pants. Clothes shopping ranks right up with a root canal for me and we had already struck out at K-Mart so I wasn't in the best of moods.

We were looking for a parking place when the incident began. In front of us was a minivan. In front of him another car which was waiting for yet another car to back out of a parking space. The minivan driver leaned on his horn. I thought to myself that's pretty rude but then it escalated. When the other car pulled into the now clear space minivan driver pulled up, rolled down his window and began yelling at the other driver.

Now this jerk was holding me up! I had important pants shopping to do! So I leaned on my horn. Maybe a little too much, if you get my drift. Mini van driver pulled ahead a few yards and then stopped. Blocking me. I threw my hands up in the in the universal, "What's the deal?" gesture and he did the same, then shook his fist at me.

We both parked and as I walked by him to get in the store he made some remark. I replied quite cleverly I thought by telling him to shut up. And so the battle was on. We traded pleasantries as we approached the store until we reached door, me first. Then I stopped abruptly and he almost walked into me. I turned around and that was the moment. I had taken all I wanted from this creep and now I was at DEF CON six and ready to paste him one on the kisser.

I really don't know what stopped me. I would like to think it was the total absurdity of the situation. I would also like to think it was my better judgment kicking in. But what I think it was that for one brief moment I saw a flash of fear in his eyes and I was back in junior high school only this time I was the bully. And I didn't like that feeling. We didn't part friends, the mean man in the minivan and I, but at least I didn't go back to junior high. *And then again I could be wrong.*

Immortality.

I sn't that what we all want in one form or another? To be remembered for something of worth long after we have shuffled off this mortal coil or whatever happens to us when we stop being alive.

Authors want to have their books live on after them. Artists want the works they paint to last forever. Parents want their children to carry on the family name proudly. Politicians want the great works they sponsor to have their names attached to them so we will always remember them for the good they did.

In the music world immortality can be a very elusive thing. I would venture to say that in music that the masters, the Beethovens and the Mozarts have probably achieved it. But in the realm of pop music very few songs are going to live forever.

But the recent death of Danny Flores brings at least one to mind that will probably be heard for time immemorial. Danny was a saxophone player in 1957 with a rockabilly group. He was playing a nameless riff in the studio when the group needed a b-side for a single. They took his riff and because he was under contract to another record label at the time listed the author as Chuck Rio. As sometimes happened back in those days of 45s the disc jockeys flipped the record over and made that b-side a number one record and gave Danny Flores his little piece of rock and roll immortality.

Danny Flores, you see was the saxophone player for the group called The Champs and also the man who shouted "Tequila" on the hit record. Danny passed away about a month ago at the age of 77. He left behind seven children, 15 grandchildren and a wife named Sharee who said at his funeral that he never tired of playing that song.

As far as a legacy goes there are worse things to be remembered for. *But then again I could be wrong.*

I read something the other day that stopped me in my tracks.

I t was in the newspaper. In just a few short words the writer summed up a feeling I have had for years. Sixteen words that describe the human condition as succinctly as almost any I have heard.

As you make your way along this path you often see moments where the only explanation is that there must be a higher power of some sort watching over us. I am not a particularly religious man but when I see puppies, a newborn baby or a pair of geese tending to their little yellow flock of hatchlings I believe in something.

It also seems like there are times when the cup of human kindness does overflow. You see moments where people do treat each other in civil ways and even heroic ways in moments where it's really called for.

There are of course always the darker moments of the soul, where pure evil is done, sometimes it seems just for evil's sake. The trial of the one man we have selected as the mastermind for 9/11 has just concluded and his sentence is to live the rest of his days in a solitary existence. It's said by some that his days are numbered. I hope that's not true and that he lives long enough to suffer daily for his abominations to mankind.

Most days we all sort of plod along, living from moment to moment trying to stay out harm's way and from doing harm to others. It seems like the very work of existing is enough. But in the laughter of a child, in the sight of a newborn colt galloping across a newly mowed pasture or a field of wildflowers waving in a spring breeze the hint of something more is there.

Oh, the words that stopped me? Sixteen of them. Here they are. A love of humanity gleams most brightly in places where it is conspicuous in its absence. Think about that the next time you're in a cancer patient's room, or a church at a funeral or a graveyard. *But then again I could be wrong.*

It looks like a tornado went through.

B ut no, it's just the road department making a total mess out of the road where I live. I lived my early years in Vermont and when I came here I looked for a place that reminded me of that. I found a beautiful hillside with a view of the unspoiled Huntsville reservoir. The road by my house is lush with evergreens and Mountain Laurel and is pretty enough for a postcard.

Usually it is, but not now. The township or somebody decided to do brush cutting. Now I understand why this is needed. The woods begin to encroach on the road and that's not good.

But you wouldn't believe the crappy job that was done. It looks like the Lake Carey shoreline after the tornados touched down. Only worse because it's mile after mile. Perfectly good trees cut down. Perfectly good trees with gashes across them that will surely kill them. Shredded tree stumps that look like a giant just twisted them off and left the splintered ends standing.

I watched these road geniuses for a while yesterday. They take a mower type deal on a hydraulic arm attached to a tractor and just slash at trees and bushes while they drive down the street. They obviously don't care what the end result looks like and they don't intend to clean up the devastation.

I went down to the road to take a closer look at what they did to the front of my property. Laying in the gully was a bird's nest with smashed eggs. Beside it was Momma Robin with a broken neck. I have to believe that there is a better way. I know the way it was done is probably cost effective and quick. It certainly isn't pretty or painless. *Or maybe I am wrong.*

It should come as no surprise to hear me say that I love music.

I love all sorts of good music. I worked in country radio for a few years and developed a taste for twang. I hosted a classical music program some years back and I can enjoy a symphony or an aria. My tastes even allow for modern jazz which when I first heard it I could not figure out but after a while I got that too. Good grief, I have even found the works of Phillip Glass – in moderation – interesting listening.

I have found over the years that others don't share my love. I can get into periods where I listen to the same song over and over again. For me this is thrilling. I dissect the tune with my ears and hear nuances and different instruments with each listen. I gather it drives those around me berserk.

Last night I woke up around 4 a.m. The road next to the house was quiet and the only other sound was my wife's steady breathing as she slumbered away. That and the sweet music of the birds. There really is no music quite like an early summer's bird chorus. The tweets are terrific. The warbles are wonderful. The chirps are….cheerful?

There are so many different bird calls. They all seem to layer over each other almost in one big song. At times it's like a call and response sort of gospel-like sound. At other moments it seems to pause and one bird will solo for a moment. I am no expert in sorting out what birds make what sounds. Oh, I can tell a blue jay from a chickadee but the sounds last night were so rich and varied I felt like a bird orchestra had gathered outside my window and in my bed I thought it was all for me. *Or then again I could be wrong.*

It smells exactly like a garbage dump.

I t actually should be somewhat nostalgic for me. I grew up in a town where you made a Saturday morning trip to the dump. Dad and I loaded up the Jeep or the station wagon with the metal cans and drove the 10 or so miles to the dump.

No fancy landfills for us. This was a stinky kind of scary place. Mounds of crap, no… mountains of crap. A somewhat frightening guy at a shack near the entrance took your $2 and you drove in. Bull dozers and road graders were spreading out the leavings of the town into an even layer or pushing it into the creek. What would an environmentalist do today? Have a heart attack probably. But we didn't know any better. So you grabbed the cans, took the lid off and tipped them upside down, giving the bottom a bang to make sure it was empty.

And the smell? There are only two smells that are like no other. Something dead in the summer heat…and a burning garbage dump. Now I get to enjoy the smell of my youth in the comfort of my own bedroom.

One of my neighbors burns trash in a 50 gallon drum. He's done it for years and it's pissed me off for years. This week has been the worst. For the past three nights he has been making a stink that smells like a crematorium. It stinks so bad you can't go out or open a window. His house is far away from the smell but mine is close and seems to always be downwind.

Some municipalities have rules about burning on your property. Some curtail the hours. Why couldn't he do it in the daytime while I am at work? All of them limit it to paper. This good neighbor evidently couldn't care less. Now I understand the need to reduce your amount of garbage. What I pay to have mine picked up is a small fortune and goes up every year. But this guy has never put his garbage out, so that means he is burning everything. Plastic milk jugs, bread wrappers, used Kleenex.

It strikes me as odd as I know he has relatives who are active in environmental causes. But he obviously comes from that group of people who feel the world is their toilet and all of us are here so they can wipe their ass with us. The obvious solution of putting some fireworks in the can has been vetoed by my wife. But it still could happen. *Or then again I could be wrong.*

It was a strange Sunday morning
and it just kept getting weirder.

S unday morning as we walked into the supermarket
some guy was backing out of a space and his car was
making a horrendous grinding noise. The long suffering
wife and I turned to see if he was dragging an old lady or
something and saw a flood of white liquid cascading out
from underneath the car. Now I know my car fluids,
having seen enough of them on the floor of my garage
from sick autos and none of them are white. As the guy
drove away nonchalant we saw the crushed plastic gallon
of milk that he had hit and run. I guess I would have
run too.

We entered the store. Thomas' Market on the
Memorial Highway is a tiny supermarket. It used to be an
Acme when my son was a bag boy. That son is 32 now.
Whew! Time flies when you are having fun.

Anyway, that section of Shavertown is real busy,
with a Burger King and McDonald's nearby, a gas station,
several car dealers and lots of homes. Urban sprawl,
northeast Pennsylvania style.

As we were nearly ready to check out I heard the
announcement over the PA. You could hear the panic in
the girl's voice as she said, "Bill to the checkouts ASAP!"

I was close enough to hear her tell Bill the
problem. It seems a deer had somehow made its way into
the store. Sure enough a young doe, according to an
eyewitness I overheard later, had navigated the highway
and the parking lot and ended up at the automatic door.
When it stepped on the activator pad the door swung
open and the deer ran inside.

I saw the poor unfortunate critter at the end of the
dairy aisle. It was having a real hard time on the shiny

linoleum floor, its hooves being designed for the woods and not grocery shopping.

It was flying around like Bambi on the ice for the first time. It would have been funny except that it wasn't. Bill and two stock boys were trying not to get a face full of sharp black hooves and were herding the doomed deer back into the stock room.

As we left I heard the same girl on the phone trying to get the game commission. The jokes would be very easy to write. But it's no joke, this event. I know it ended badly for the lost deer. And I know as we take more and more of the woods where Bambi should live and make them into grocery stores and fast food joints that this sort of outcome is going to occur more often. Soon it will be as common as road kill. *Or then again I could be wrong.*

It was the beginning of the end for me.

The end of innocence and the beginning of my lifetime distrust of those in power and their ability to use that power to good purposes.

I was 17-years-old when the National Guard opened fire. I would graduate high school that year and head off to college in Boston, a big adventure for a hick kid from Vermont. As I remember the day I was probably in class around the time the order to fire on Kent State University students was given.

In that day of less than instant communication, I don't think I would have learned about the cold-blooded killing of four until the nightly news with Walter Cronkite. I do remember seeing footage of the massacre. Well not of the actual shooting, but of the protest marchers and the troops gathered. I remember thinking of how odd that sight was juxtaposed with the footage of the Vietnam War. Here were fighting men in the jungle getting killed and there were college students protesting and also getting killed. In my 17-year-old brain it didn't compute. And it still doesn't.

On May 4, 1970, the Ohio National Guard opened fire into a college campus during a school day. A total of 67 shots were fired in 13 seconds. Four students were killed. Nine students were wounded.

And now after all these years and tears and denials and accusations, the smoking gun has surfaced. The smoking gun in the form of an audio tape that seems to prove what I and my generation have known for 37 years. The tape which is noisy and hard to understand nonetheless has the voice, some say of a National Guard officer giving the command. *"Right here. Get set. Point. Fire."* And four were dead in Ohio.

People ask me why I am so cynical about the government. Why I have nothing but disdain for the lunacy that puts our young generations in harm's way year after year.

If you need to know the source of my complete and utter mistrust of the powerful just look at the image of that day. A young girl with her face contorted in anguish looking at the dead body of a fellow student on the ground on a college campus. It's an image seared into my brain forever and it changed me.

And now to go along with that black and white photo I have the sound of someone in charge giving the order to kill young people. Don't ask me why I have no faith in the government. My faith died that spring day in May. And nothing that has happened since has proven me wrong.

It was the oddest house sale I have ever been to.

A nd I have seen a few. The signs were everywhere in the Dallas, Pennsylvania area. Fluorescent bright, they had loads of information on them printed in itsy bitsy little printing that you had to stop the car to read. Long on the items being sold the signs which seemed to be on every phone pole were very short on directions. But we found the joint.

Thus the saga of horror began. As it often the case in these house sales this one was being held because someone died and the survivors want to clean out the house prior to selling it. So they open all the closets, dump out all the drawers and throw price tags on everything in the hopes that people like me will buy the stuff and save them carting it out to a dumpster.

In this case it was obvious mom had died. My first tip off was the fact that the floral arrangement that had obviously been on the casket, you know the one that says "Mom" on it was in the front yard. No price tag on that one but I bet if you asked....well.

Undaunted by this we went in. It was a typical old lady's house in this area, with typical old lady stuff. One room had a door sign that read, and I am not making this up, "Price on items is not right." Ok. This room really had no floor, covered with every imaginable item you can think of and several you can't. One corner had loads of small porcelain and glass figurines which my long suffering wife has an eye for. She spent the better part of 10 minutes to clear a path to these only to have a large smelly man jump in front of her.

It was at this point I left to go outside to look at the flowers that were on mom's casket for a while. I felt guilty and went back in. My wife had finally made it to the figurines and there was steam coming off her. One of the family came in to help clear off the counter where my wife was looking. She picked up a box with about 1,000 push pins inside and dropped these in an even layer all over the floor. I went back outside.

The third time I came back in I joined my bride in the kitchen. A family member about six foot three was in there with us. He was wearing a hunter orange vest, at least a four day growth of beard and a somewhat deranged look on his face. He looked right at me and pretty much shouted, "What are you doing here?"

I really had no answer. Was I in the wrong house? Was the kitchen off limits?

I went back outside to look at the flowers. A few people came up to me while I was standing there and asked if there was good stuff inside. I said there were loads of pushpins. They gave me odd looks. I said you probably could get a deal on these flowers. *But then again I could be wrong.*

B ut boy, what a difference it can make. I live for the weekend that we turn the clocks back. On the other side of that coin I hate it when we jump forward. I have always been an early riser. Whether this has anything to do with my name or not I am unsure but getting up at 5 a.m. or even earlier is not a big deal to me. I also am one of those insufferable people who jump out of bed awake and usually in a pretty good mood. I also have the ability to set an internal alarm clock and wake up when I tell myself to.

All of this changes the day we set the clocks back. I feel that I have been robbed and it throws my system out of whack completely. That's why this past weekend I look forward to that extra little hour. It makes my life balance out and I feel like I am getting back what I am owed.

Changing the clocks has always been my job around the house. It was one of those things my dad always did and I have to uphold the male tradition, right? It used to be a real chore. Especially the VCR and other electronic clocks. The procedure was to try for 10 or 15 minutes to do it from memory. *Ah ha ha ha*, it's to laugh. Then another 10 or 15 minute search for the instruction manual. I do have every manual for everything I have ever bought neatly filed. That's the problem. I have never thrown one of these manuals out even though the device has long since gone to that great device heaven. So I wade through the stacks of these manuals, usually printed in at least three languages until I found the right one.

Last year we upgraded to a new VCR/DVD player in the bedroom and a Tivo in the living room. I searched for and found the manuals and sat down on Sunday morning to wrestle with the clocks. I looked at the manual for half an hour to discover that the darn things had already done the job for me. Same thing with my new fangled cell phone. I even managed to call tech support before I noticed that I was an unnecessary part of this equation. These things will take care of themselves even when I am long gone to my reward.

Except the bird clock. You have one of these, right? Or something like it I am sure. It, on the hour, sings or plays music or sounds like a motorcycle. The trick is to get it in synch so it plays the right bird at the right hour. Not an easy task since I can readily identify two out of 12 bird calls on that sucker. So I guess that I still serve a function here. Twice a year anyway. *And then again I could be wrong.*

It's a little like seeing someone naked that you really don't want to.

T he first few days of decent weather after a long hard cold northeast Pennsylvania winter are a mixed blessing. I love the feeling that we have emerged from a cave, blinking into the sunlight like bears after a long hibernation.

This winter for some reason seems like it has always been here. But the snow leaving the ground uncovers all sorts of nasty stuff. It's a bit like seeing your parents naked. You know you shouldn't be seeing it but it grabs your eye...and then you are sorry.

Travel any stretch of northeast roadway now. I commute on the Cross Valley Expressway and a short distance on I-81 north. The amount and diversity of crap on the roadside is astounding. The mounds of snow have receded leaving everything you might expect and a few things that boggle the mind. An empty case that once held an expensive imported beer. If you could afford to buy that brand why couldn't you find a place to throw it away? Hundreds of thousands of coffee cups. An interesting survey could be done to find out the most popular java. Same for soda and beer empties. I once mentioned to a distributor of Coors that I saw more of his empties on the roadside than any other brand. I did mean it as a compliment but he gave me a funny look. I get a lot of funny looks so I don't worry about them so much anymore.

And the soda bottles! Some that are full of what looks like ice tea? Truckers don't like to stop and go... so they drain the soda and re-fill on the run. *Eeewh!* I have heard that the guys who pick up roadside litter find this so disgusting that they are demanding hazard pay. Even worse than road kill. The poor slobs who run the mowers on the median strip must have to wear wet suits. Imagine the explosion of trucker pee when the blades of one of those huge mowers hits it! Gusher! I guess I can understand the trucker's reluctance to stop. And I think I know why they just toss it. Picture the trucker walking to a garbage can with a full bottle of his golden output. But there must be a better solution.

And the road kill? I like to try and guess what it was. Skunks and deer are easy. It's the ones that have been mashed into pancake thin layers that keep me intrigued.

Sometimes when some idiot has crashed and I get stuck for what seems like an eternity waiting for the highway to clear I look out the side window and try to figure out the back story of some of the debris. An entire screen door. Did it fall off a manufactured house? The top to a beverage cooler. Was it in the back of a pick-up truck and the wind took it? One shoe. Why just one? Condoms. Used. That just baffles me completely. I can only hope that it was backseat passengers engaging in a little mobile loving. The other alternative...well I am having more than a little trouble figuring that one out. At least the sex was safe!

Soon the PennDOT workers or whoever it is that gets the nasty job of sprucing up the shoulders will be back on the case. Hundreds of trash bags stuffed to the max with all of the above will appear and for a short while it will look....sort of clean and pristine. It's just a sure sign that spring is in the air. And on the roadways of northeast Pennsylvania.

It's beginning to look a lot like Christmas.

P eople who drive once a year to buy presents for the great grandkids are on the road. Mother Nature dumps rain, snow, sleet, ice on us. Long lines everywhere.

A couple of days ago I had to go and mail the packages to the out of state relatives. My long suffering wife buys the stuff, wraps the gifts, packs them in the boxes and the least I can do is take them to be mailed, right? Four big heavy boxes. Really big heavy boxes. Did I mention heavy? I have sent them by UPS the past few years. I have noticed that this is getting to be a less than pleasant process. Now I am not blaming the rank and file at the counter at the local UPS terminal. They are great...patient under pressure, cheerful and hardworking guys. But the big wheels at UPS have made it harder every year.

First it was long lines in the warehouse...which worked ok. Then they shut the warehouse and put this process in an office twice the size of a phone booth. Two guys behind the counter. Then it was one guy. Then the hours were cut from 9-7 p.m. to 11 a.m.-7 p.m. Now it's 3-7 p.m. So the crush that was in many more hours now is condensed to FOUR HOURS!

And some genius decided this year it would all be computerized. Only they didn't tell you when you got in the phone booth with 50 other unhappy people with 600 packages that the first step was to print your label on the computer. So after waiting in line for an hour (don't forget the four HEAVY packages) you get told, no you have to go back to the beginning of THAT line! Then get your labels and stand in line again! AAAAHHH! Did I mention that all this time you are trying to herd four big HEAVY packages? With 50 other people trying to do the same thing?

I gave up. Lugged the four big HEAVY packages back out to the car. I went to the Luzerne, Pennsylvania post office. No line. No computer. Just a nice man named Jim who took my four big heavy packages with a smile and sent them on their way. Had a nice Grinch tie on too.

It's hot.

A frica hot. I don't like the heat. One time I was offered a job in Florida, a pretty good job as a matter of fact. My long suffering wife just looked at me and said, "You wouldn't last a month in that heat." And she was right of course, as usual. "If you can't stand the heat, get out of the kitchen. Give 'em hell," Harry Truman said.

I remember when I was a kid that the hot weather didn't seem to bother me as much. Of course as a kid I spent every waking summer moment in a swimsuit at the local municipal pool or else submerged in a lake so I don't think I knew it was hot. Hot enough for you? I would be spending just as much time in my swimming pool at home but the storm with no name did it in and so no swimming for Jim this year. Don't get hot under the collar.

We have one air conditioner in the house and several fans. The A.C. is in the bedroom and does a fabulous job of cooling down that small room. As long as you keep the door shut and the unit on Armageddon setting. The fans, two floor models and one ceiling fan do a fabulous job of moving around hot air. I think they actually make the air hotter and then blow it at you.

My house was built long before anyone thought too much about the heat. I really don't know what they did back then when it got hot. Probably the same thing I am doing now. Complain. "It ain't the heat; it's the humility," as Yogi Berra said.

The windows in the living room can't take a full-size air conditioner due to the fact that they have little decorative shutters indoors that don't open wide enough for one. Don't ask why I don't just take them off.

If you think that is a solution then A: you are not married and B: see A.

We spent yesterday driving around town looking at portable air conditioners. These things look like small refrigerators on wheels and cost as much as my first car. They still need to be vented which means you connect them with a dryer hose to a window. Some of them need a drain pipe for the water they make. It looks like a pain and we didn't get one. Yet.

The seven day forecast calls for 97 degrees tomorrow. And it's not even 8 a.m. as I write these words and it's already 80 degrees in the kitchen. "If you saw a heat wave, would you wave back?" So asks Steven Wright. *Or then again I could be wrong.*

Modern life has all sorts of interesting ways to stress you out that our ancestors didn't have to deal with.

When Og the caveman had a dispute with somebody he clobbered them over the head with his trusty club and then they were gone. No more dispute. Nowadays of course we are more civilized and instead of clubs we use...lawyers.

Twenty years ago I had the unhappy experience of going through a divorce. Kids were involved so there were seemingly endless meetings with domestic relations and lawyers were always part of the festivities. My ex-wife chose a legal beagle that I now see almost every day.

Now I am sure this is a highly qualified member of the bar. I am positive that he does his job well and is a credit to his profession. I know the fact that he made me crazy back then is my fault and none of his. But I didn't care for him then and I haven't warmed to him since.

So why do I see him everyday? Well I don't see him in person. I see his 14 foot high mug on billboards all over town. And I must say he looks the same as he did 20 years ago. And he still raises my blood pressure when I look at his unsmiling face. It takes me right back to those less than pleasant days when I was chewed up and spit out by a legal system endorsed by the Commonwealth.

The last time I saw this guy the most vivid memory I took away was the layer of egg he had on his tie. Of course I left those meetings with empty pockets and egg on my face so who came out better? You have to wonder. What would Og the caveman have done. Put another way. WWOD. What would Og do? *Or then again I could be wrong.*

My dog died a few years back and that's why I have a dumpster in my yard.

I t's also indirectly why I move like a very old man today and also why I need some time off. My Siberian passed on a few years ago. Nikiya was an "outdoor" dog who never liked being inside so we set her up in a storage shed with a dog house inside. Took the door off and put her on a lead with a pulley rig and she had loads of shade and a pretty good doggy life. Nikiya was tough! She would take her doggy water dish on below freezing days and throw it at some cinder blocks and then chew the ice up. She would just look up at me, as if saying, "What?"

After she died I must admit I wasn't emotionally able to do much with "her" shed. The roof caved in last year. The floor rotted out and the thing was an eyesore, even though you really can't see it all that well because of the overgrowth. You get the picture. It had to go.

I hired a guy to pull it down. He said, "Get a dumpster." I called up my buddy in the dumpster business and he had one the size of the Queen Mary II set down in my yard. It's bigger than my garage.

So I'm looking at this huge thing and I had a brainstorm. Why not...clean out the attic? It won't take that long and we can get rid of all this useless clutter. My attic runs the whole length of the house and is big enough to stand in. It was so completely full that you couldn't walk in it without piles of stuff falling.

So bright and early Saturday morning I tackled the first of the job. An old box spring and mattress...why we saved it, I'll never know. Wrestled it down the stairways and tossed it into the Queen Mary. *Wow!* That felt great! That was easy! Let's get moving.

Ten hours later we gave up. Oh, we did yeoman's work. But it was overwhelming. What was in there? An air conditioner from my first house. The size of a Buick. Does it work? Yes, but it leaks water badly. *BAM!* into the now building heap. Two VCRs that were classified "not worth fixing" by the repairman. Twenty years of jackets and sweaters and shirts and pants that are so out of style and so worn out that even I can't bear to take them to the Salvation Army. Cassettes. I have worked in radio all my life and I must have saved every cassette that I was sent. Most with only one song. Video tapes with just one song on them. Literally thousands of them. Save them? For what? *BAM!*

And boxes. Boxes from every piece of technology we have purchased in the last two decades. Boxes for TVs. Boxes for answering machines we don't own anymore. Boxes for VCRs and DVD players that broke. Boxes from Christmas shipments past. Boxes with boxes IN them. And of course all these boxes have Styrofoam packing or foam peanuts or what we used to call excelsior stuffed in them.. All those boxes had to be made to lie flat in the dumpster. I lost some blood in that process from staples hooking me.

Up and down the stairs. Down the front yard hill (slipping and falling because of course it started to rain). Back and forth.

About eight hours in, I discovered my car had a flat, so I pumped it up and drove over to Jack Williams. I was wearing a pair of sweat pants that were more hole than pant. A t-shirt that could walk on its own (Smell bad? That doesn't describe it). My arms were covered with blood from the staples trying to kill me. My oldest sneakers. And the sneakers? Don't forget I have been "playing" in a dumpster with inches of rainwater in it. To put it politely "dumpster juice" soaked into the sneakers. I was in a pretty bad mood, unshaved and uncombed. As the song goes: "My feet stink and I don't love Jesus."

The guys at Jack Williams couldn't have been nicer but the place was jumping. They said they would get to me as soon as they could but, "please bear with them." Ok. I sat down in the waiting area. Read the newspaper.

A small boy came in with his dad and the kid sat down next to me. For about a minute. Looked like he was going to puke and moved way off. Telling his Dad loudly, "That man stinks!" They got me out of there in record time! I don't think I was helping business.

My long suffering wife claims that I used to dance to the Billy Ray Cyrus song "Achy Breaky Heart."

I deny this but I know she doesn't lie so I can only assume there was alcohol involved. I am not a big fan of country music. I like it about as much as I like kielbasa which is to say in small doses with lots of time in between usage.

I also did not care for Billy Ray Cyrus in his first incarnation. He kind of creeped me out be honest with that mullet hair and all those muscles. But my wife and her sister like the guy so in order to earn some brownie points (I am a little short on points lately. My behavior tends to earn me cold shoulders and acid tongues but that's another rant.)

I made it possible to see him at Penn's Peak in Jim Thorpe last Friday. Because of my connections I was also able to get them in close proximity to him backstage. More on that later.

Penn's Peak deserves a solid A+ as a concert venue. Over the years I have seen a few shows, in more than a few places, some good, some not so much. This place is designed perfectly with crystal clear sound, a comfortable uncrowded seating arrangement and an unbelievably helpful and friendly staff. I have seen several shows there and each experience has been better than the previous.

I didn't expect to come away liking Billy Ray Cyrus any better but as it turns out (and it usually does) I was wrong. Billy Ray has had his career ups and downs. When you begin a career with a chart buster like "Achy Breaky Heart" you often get pigeonholed in the music biz as a novelty act. Credit Cyrus with perseverance and talent as he has had many hits and continues to perform sold-out shows each year.

Backstage with a huge group of fans before the show he was friendly and courteous to a fault. Friday was his 45th birthday so he was getting loads of presents from everyone including a cowboy hat with Harley Davidson decorations from my wife's sister. She, all knowing person that she is, had inside knowledge of Billy's Harley ownership and as it turns out she was right. Low and behold, Billy took the stage and by the second song he had the crowd in the palm of his hand and the gifted Harley hat on his head.

A few other things worth recounting. A song about veterans was preceded by an emotional speech by Billy Ray about his recently deceased dad and how this was his first birthday without a call from him. You could have heard a pin drop.

And near to us during the show was a Vietnam vet who was thrilled to pieces to be seeing Billy Ray. He threw his beaded necklace on stage telling me this was a special reminder of his days "in-country." Billy Ray picked it up and put it on. I have seen happy people in my life but not quitelike that 'Nam vet that night. His smile could have lit the night up for 50 miles.

As a result of my night with Billy Ray, I still probably won't be dancing sober to "Achy Breaky Heart." But I came away with nothing but respect for a guy who now looks more like Kurt Cobain with his long non-mullet hair and a small soul patch then a muscle-bound Camaro owner. Oh, and I think I earned a couple of brownie points. *But then again I could be wrong.*

Now I have nothing against teenage girls.

T hey are fun to look at – from a distance – and they have many endearing qualities. Belly shirts and flipping their hair behind their ears and giggling among them.

But a bunch of teen girls running a business is a recipe for disaster. It's pretty hard to screw up selling ice cream. I mean the premise is so extraordinarily easy that you wouldn't think you could do too much to make it go badly. You would be wrong.

The gaggle of teenage pups behind the counter of the dairy store were inattentive at best, and sort of rude at their worst. It's not that we aren't clear when we order. Oh, no. We have learned to almost spell it out. One of my family likes a banana split. The proper way to have it made is with three scoops of ice cream. Vanilla, chocolate and strawberry. Then you put the strawberry sauce over the strawberry and vanilla and the hot fudge over the chocolate. Whipped cream, dry walnuts and a cherry. Think you could get it that way? *Ahahah*, it's to laugh. The topping part is the hardest apparently. It's never right.

This past weekend brought a new wrinkle. The concept of strawberry ice cream eluded our young blonde server. I tasted and I am still not sure what flavor it was other than that it was not strawberry. Many times one key ingredient will elude them. I guess it's easy to forget why you call it a banana split. But shouldn't it really have a banana in their somewhere?

My taste is for a hot fudge sundae. This time I got it exactly right. Never mind the big dollop of fudge on the outside on the dish. The fact that my teenage server wiped it off with a finger and then licked it probably should have been charming or cute or sexy or something. I guess.

I am thinking that this summer job isn't exactly what our teen queens had in mind. A budding doctor or CEO must find it so demeaning. I am sure it's not much fun. And I am sure that they will find a way to make sure that next summer they are doing something that will better mankind.

As sure as I am that there will be another crop of oh-so-cute, not-so-bright, borderline rude adolescents to take their place. *Or then again I could be wrong.*

I've had some pretty crappy jobs in my life.

E ven though most of my jobs have been in radio (and some of those were pretty crappy to be honest about it, but that's a whole different story), I did as a youngster hold several unpleasant jobs.

There was the brief but memorable three days as a dishwasher at a white table cloth restaurant. I was all of 15 and at that stage where just handling other people's discarded food was enough to make me gag. The huge dishwashing machine scared the hell out me. I still remember the big red letters "Hobart" on that sucker. And my boss in the kitchen was a toothless old derelict named Sammy who basically scrubbed pots and told me what to do. Like I say I lasted only three days before I called in sick for the rest of my life.

Then there was the bookstore job at the local college. How bad could it be? How about unloading tractor trailer loads full of books. Hundreds of trailers, millions of books. Did you know books in quantity are real heavy? Take my word on it.

Then there was the guy who hired me to clean his basement but really wanted me to clean his personal basement if you know what I mean. I never ran so fast in my life after I figured out his angle. Now we would have him locked up, but back then I just left in a hurry.

But as lousy as those jobs were I can't imagine being the obit editor on call Christmas day. What brings this to mind is a brief notice in the paper the other day. The item, slugged "Holiday Deadline" (and that seems really ironic) explained that the deadline on Christmas day to submit obituaries is 9 p.m.

It's a well know fact that lots of folks drop dead on Christmas day. In dead-on-arrival emergency departments and outpatient groups, more cardiac deaths occurred on December 25 than on any other day of the year. The second-largest number of deaths was on December 26, and the third-largest number was on January 1. Speculation is it may be because people, many senior citizens, are delaying getting medical treatment because of the holidays.

But back to the obit desk at the newspaper. How does it feel to pick up the phone and take down the details of someone's passing on Christmas day? As if it's not bad enough that while everyone else is eating turkey and watching the Eagles play the Cowboys you are working but you are also sitting waiting to hear about some poor family's misery. And until 9 p.m. yet. So let's raise a mug of holiday cheer for the loneliest guy (or gal) in the world on Christmas day. The obit writer on call. *Or then again I could be wrong.*

Parking lots shouldn't cause your blood pressure to rise.

W hat is it with some people and parking lots? The spaces are clearly marked at one place where I park daily. It's a medium-sized lot that is never full but gets crowded in front of the business I frequent. Why does this person who parks every day ignore the lines? They consistently park with the line running right down the middle of their behemoth-mobile SUV effectively taking up two parking spaces. In fact because there are two rows of spaces and they park in the middle of the two rows they eat up four spaces.

And another thing. Why do people speed in parking lots? Ever see that *National Lampoon's Vacation* movie? There is a scene in there where Chevy Chase is driving the family truckster sound asleep on a sidewalk at high speed. A guy walks out of a door and is almost clobbered by the car. That's the way it looks to me as I watch some people at racing speed in the narrow rows of some lots. If you walk out from between cars you may become another notch on their grill. What would it say on your tombstone? Flattened at Wal-Mart?

And why is it so important to get that space? I have fallen into this kind of behavior myself. You see someone vacating a space. You wait patiently with your blinker on while they back out. Someone zooms into space before you. I have seen fights erupt over this. Why? It's just a parking space? Why does it make us so furious?

All these things I have mentioned. They increase exponentially at Christmas time. If you're counting, it's 128 days. *And about that I am not wrong.* But write me anyway.

If you scratch me underneath all the
layers you will find a radio broadcaster.

S o it is when one of our club passes on I think a bit about this business, why we lunatics are in it and how it has changed.

When I first came to this area about 25 years ago WNAK was even then considered a bit odd in this business. It was owned and operated by one, Bob Neilson, a man I never had the pleasure of meeting.

The station was just plain old. It played old music, sounded old and tired even back then. It obviously was almost a one man band. Bob did lengthy commentaries, everything moved slowly and the effect was you were listening to a throwback to a time when radio receivers were the size of refrigerators and the pace of life was more relaxed.

And the music…a real hodgepodge of Big Band, sludgy instrumentals and what we used to call middle of the road vocalists: Perry Como, Bing Crosby, Rosemary Clooney. Not much Sinatra though, because as I understood it Bob didn't like his alleged mob connections. WNAK played hymns on Sunday and not much else. For a time I don't think they even played commercials on the Sabbath. Another one of Bob's beliefs.

One very memorable rating book WNAK beat all stations in the ratings aged 12 and older. Sure it was mostly persons aged 50 plus but to a young broadcaster it was a slap in the face and a call to arms. Tapes were made of the 730 AM signal and rushed to consultants all over America. One called me up and said, "Very funny. Now send us the real tapes." No, that's how it sounded.

I once remarked that WNAK was playing the same records that it signed on with in the early decades of radio. Not just the same songs but the same old scratchy records.

But you have to admire guys like Bob Neilson. They had a vision, did it their way and never compromised, even when he had to resort to begging on the air for money to pay the light bill.

We don't see many stand alone operators in radio nowadays. And we see damn few who do anything but cookie cutter copies of what works elsewhere.

So it is with the perspective of my decreasing distance from my own sign-off that I present this brief mention of a local radio legend to you. Robert Neilson, previously of WNAK 730 Broadcasters, "signed-off" to be with the Lord on Sunday, March 13, 2005. A service was held with full military honors at Indiantown Gap V.A. National Cemetery.

Remember juke boxes?

S ure you do. You put a quarter in for three plays and the thing grabbed an actual record and played it. Some places had little remote boxes at your table where you could flip through the cards and pick out your songs.

Here's a little known but true fact. Top 40 radio was designed after a guy sitting in a bar noticed that people played the same songs over and over again on the juke box. He figured the same thing would work on the radio and voila a format was born out of repetitiveness.

But that was then, this is now. Nowadays juke boxes are all stocked with CDs and you can play entire albums. And even more amazing they now have juke boxes that are somehow wired into the internet so they can literally play any song at anytime. This is too good to pass up.

What I am about to suggest is not a good idea. You might get into a fight by doing this. I would suggest that you not listen to what I am about to tell you, if you ever see one of these internet connected juke boxes. But it might be a pretty funny way to spend an hour at a bar. If you see one of these high tech jukes at the local watering hole...and I think there's one at the Bennigan's near the arena in Wilkes-Barre, whatever you do don't do the following. Ask it to find and play a "song" by Brian Eno called "Thursday Afternoon."

I just read an article in the Sunday magazine from the *New York Times* to give credit where credit is due where someone did just that. And it almost caused a riot.

Brian Eno is a composer and producer who has worked with a bunch of bands including U2, and most recently Paul Simon. When he is on his own he composes what is called ambient music. It is music only in the sense that it uses instruments. It's not what you would call toe-tapping good time stuff. In fact, it's painful to listen to in short bursts.

And here's the funny thing about this whole deal. Brian Eno's "Thursday Afternoon" is a collection of random noises, ethereal tings and washes of synthesized sounds sort of like waves. It goes on for 61 minutes.

By all accounts it produces some pretty ugly moods in a bar where you might hear Toby Keith or C&C Music Factory. And it's sort of like holding the whole place hostage for more than an hour.

Again with the disclaimer. Don't do this. But if you do, let me know where and when. I might want to stop on by and watch the fun. If I can find my earplugs. *Or then again I could be wrong.*

So the biggest news according to a local newspaper is that there will be beer to drink in Kirby Park during the Fourth of July holiday.

F ront page news that is. This follows a week of screaming headlines that the big name act that will be entertaining us on July 3rd will be the has-been group, the Beach Boy.

Oh, I know they are supposed to be called the Beach Boys but it's really not you know. The only real member of the original Beach Boys on tour these days is Cousin Mike Love. The brothers Wilson, two thirds of whom are dead and one who is as crazy as a outhouse rat will not be celebrating with a cool frosty one come the endless summer in Wilkes-Barre. Mike Love is 65 now. He probably won't be too worried about much surfing these days.

And that kind of is the crux of the matter for me. The best we can do, the biggest thing we can provide for entertainment for the reported half million bucks Wilkes-Barre is dishing out for the festivities is beer and the Beach Boy?

The downtown's biggest problem right now is that no one, especially young people give a rat's pattootie about it. There is nothing for them and it's not too pretty. So the solution is suds and fossils on stage?

It sort of reminds me of the brief radio career of David Lee Roth. Some dumb radio exec (and believe me there is no shortage of those in my business) probably heard the name and recognized it. Roth lasted only a few weeks on the air because he was terrible. Some Wilkes-Barre exec, also no stranger to dumb in that group, heard the Beach Boys and said, "Yeah, I know them." And the deal was done.

I saw the Beach Boys in Scranton, 22-some-odd years ago when they actually had more than one original member. They were off key, painfully dull and did the shortest set I had ever seen. I am willing to bet that the Beach Boy will not be a whole lot better.

I just checked Pollstar to see who else might be available this summer. John Prine, John Hiatt, Government Mule, Bruce Hornsby, Heart, James Brown, Kansas, The New Cars and Blondie pop out to me. I am pretty sure you could book three or four of those acts for what we will pay the Beach Boy. But some old farts wouldn't recognize the names.

And so we get what we always get here in the valley with a heart. Washed-out, has-been, and overpriced. And don't get me started about opening act, Dakota. *Or then again I could be wrong.*

So the new Wilkes-Barre/Scranton International Airport terminal will be open soon and boy, I can't wait.

W aves of prosperity will soon wash over our area like a tsunami in Asia, all because we the taxpayers have dumped $41.5 into the sky port.

At least that's what the big wheels at the airport are hoping and wishing for. Of course the airport guys never met my father who used to say wish in one hand and go to the bathroom in the other and see what you have. He said it sort of like that anyway. Boy, I sure hope it does crank up the local economy. It sure isn't working so good now.

So far in 2006, the airport has been like an albatross around our necks. The dead loss so far this year? Near 70 thousand bucks. That's more than a quarter of a million dollars a year if it continues to bleed money at the current rate. If we lose that much money for 160 years then we will have lost as much as it took to build the Wilkes-Barre/Scranton International Airport and School of Truck Driving.

But the wise wheels at the Wilkes-Barre/Scranton International Airport Bar and Grill and Art Display have chosen a particularly auspicious time to open the doors on the grand new aviation palace. Gas prices, and that's what those jet airplanes guzzle, are climbing faster than the space shuttle in launch mode. Inflation is killing all of us, people are terrified to fly after 9/11 and we have seen at least two alleged airlines go belly up after a few flights in and out of the Wilkes-Barre/Scranton International House of Pancakes and Aviation.

I have talked to some pilots who fly into and out of our little local airport. Oddly enough from the pilots perspective the terminal was the least of the problem here. They were more concerned about vectors and short runways and such. I bet if you asked a pilot what 41 million bucks should have been spent on he might have mentioned that fact that the control tower and associated radar and communications devices have been around since "Lucky Lindy" landed the *Spirit of St Louis* in a field in our area in ought 27. Ok, I exaggerate. A little.

But when you have spent 1.2 million dollars on the front door to the joint, don't you think a little money could have thrown into pothole patching on the runways? *But then again I could be wrong.*

***Sometimes I feel like the world is an
elaborate stage set made just for me.***

D id you ever doubt that you were real? I sometimes
do. I feel like I am invisible or just that no one
notices me. Happens a lot when I am trying to signal
waiters in a restaurant to bring me another drink. But
that's another story.

Sometimes I will wake up in the night and I will
be convinced that there is nothing out there. Nothing at
all, a darkness a vacuum. I am afraid to step to the
window to see if I am right.

Sometimes when I close my eyes when I am out in
the world, in the instant that I open them it seems as
though everything was put back in place just in time.

I watched the lunar landing as a kid. I was ill with
a high fever and in and out of consciousness – a pretty
serious illness. But Mom parked me in front of the TV
and I saw the live pictures of Neil Armstrong's putting his
foot on the moon. I know that once when I opened my
eyes I saw a large, hairy hand put the lunar module back
in place.

Some would say this betrays a indulgent view of
the universe, an inability to think of myself as anything
but the center of all creation. I think I am just seeing
clearly. What do you think?

***Someone asked me the other day if this was the most
fun I have ever had working at a radio station.***

I had to think for a minute and my answer may
surprise some of you. I said, "No."
I have been in radio for over 35 years, most of
which have been fun. I have had the opportunity to help
birth more than a dozen radio stations in my career. My
on-air work has allowed me to do many exciting things,
from pilot a nuclear sub to broadcast live from a stock car
while I raced on an oval track. I have the tape of that
broadcast somewhere. It features a very loud engine, and
at one point my terrified sounding voice says "I think I
sh&* myself!"
I have made many friends in this business and met
so many stars that it would take pages to list them all. My
wife keeps a scrapbook of all this stuff. Actually she is on
scrapbook number six at this time. It kind of
embarrasses me but it's cool anyway.
I have also worked at some real terrible places.
The station in Jacksonville, North Carolina that sent me
to bar remote night out. The stage had (honest) chicken
wire between the performers and the bar proper. Just like
that scene in the *Blues Brothers* movie, the crowd threw
beer bottles at me all night.
Then there was the alcoholic, drug-addled
general manger who made my life miserable for six
months and then was too cowardly to fire me face-to-face
but instead had his wife do it! Right Mike?
The most fun I ever had in radio? The first job. I
was working in an industry that I was learning to love. I
didn't know anything and I was learning on the job. It
was intimidating, exciting and FUN!

*Sometimes a cow has to do what a cow has to do
and it doesn't matter what the situation is.*

L ast Saturday, I spent a most pleasant day at The
Lands at Hillside Farms enjoying the spring
festival. You probably heard about it, a big fund raiser for
the non-profit group that has taken over the huge farm
and dairy store and are trying very hard to both keep it
running and in some cases to return it to what it should
be, a working dairy farm.

Among other things planned for the many acres
are a fine dining restaurant, a bed and breakfast and a
home for free range cattle. It's going to take a lot of work
sweat and tears but if Saturday's event was any measure
they will get the job done and more. It was a great event
filled with arts and crafts booths, a wonderful smelling
food tent stuffed with all sorts of delicious things like pies
and fudges and all the things my endless diet won't allow
me to sample.

I was in charge of the PA system and spent the day
working with the musicians who played the wildest
variety of instruments I have ever been associated with
and that is saying a lot. Let's just say it's the first time I
have ever placed a microphone on a handsaw being used
as a musical instrument and leave it at that.

The day's events included the usual raffles and
other fund raisers but the one everyone seemed to have
the most interest in was the kiss the cow contest. Several
of the organizers of the event had volunteered or more
likely were guilt-tripped into kissing a bovine if they so to
speak won the contest. People voted by making
a donation.

All in good fun except I don't think they asked the
cow about the deal. The cow in question was a baby calf

143

and was adorable in the way that all baby animals are. All legs and big brown eyes it was so cute you wanted to hug it. Kissing it not so much.

But the competition ended and the big cheese won, a man named Andy Check. The little calf named Abbie was brought front and center and as the crowd watched Andy delivered the smooch square on the cow's kisser. I had a great view of what happened next as I was behind the line of fire. It happened so fast after the kiss on the bovine lips that it couldn't have possibly been a coincidence. The little calf lifted its tail and as they say what goes in comes out.

Not to be indelicate about it and really how can you be at this point Abbie, the recently kissed cow, voted twice. Andy put on a brave act but deep down you could tell that the rejection hurt his feelings. I mean if that's what a cow does after a kiss from Andy, how does his wife react? *Or then again I could be wrong.*

Sometimes you have to wonder about the thought processes that go on in our rulers' minds.

R ecently there has been much discussion about pay phones in downtown Wilkes-Barre, Pennsylvania. The problem is that drug dealers and prostitutes allegedly are using the phones in the pursuit of their professions.

I can't dispute this. I don't know any drug dealers or ladies of the night to ask and I certainly am not going to hang around those phones in the name of research if you get my drift. So city council in our fair metropolis has met to discuss the issue and initially came up with a proposal to nuke all the phones. Just rip the suckers right out of the ground and let the creepy crawliest as Jim McCarthy calls'em find another way to communicate.

The problem is that the street business people get very angry when you take away what they consider their offices and take it out on the local business.

A while back the A-Plus store in South Wilkes-Barre yanked their outside phones and ended up with a bunch of hostile characters demanding to use the store's phone and getting rowdy when refused.

So A-Plus got the idea of putting the phones back in and installing video cameras. So if the police are serious about wanting to stop the creepy crawliest all they need do is borrow the video and talk to the frequent stars of the show.

According to the A-Plus store manager the police have never asked for the tapes even though he was sure they knew they existed.

So the question is why? Which is better? Taking all the pay phones out and inconveniencing the people who need them for legitimate uses, or installing video surveillance on the ones you suspect might be trouble and using the tapes to track down the criminals?

It seems like a no brainier to me. And I guess that's why as poor as I am in that department I am overqualified for community leadership. *Or then again I could be wrong.*

Sooner or later, it had to happen.

My town is getting a Starbucks. I will admit here and now that I have only had one cup of Starbucks coffee in my life.

I was at a business meeting in Chicago which promised to be a long and probably pretty boring affair. Two of my fellow business meeting goers suggested a quick run to Starbucks to fuel up on expensive caffeine. Not knowing how or what to order I let the other guys order for me. When I was handed the cup I took the top off and put my usual three packets of artificial sweetener in it. The other guys just looked on with shock and informed me that the coffee was already plenty sweet. So I had a really really sweet cup of Starbucks coffee. It sucked. But that was my fault, not Starbucks.

Starbucks must have something going for it. The chain, which has been around since 1971, has 12,000 locations in at least 30 countries and has over 117,000 people on the payroll. Some say a town isn't truly considered to be completely civilized until you have at least one Starbucks.

So now Dallas, Pennsylvania will be completely civilized. Why is it then that I think it would be equally important to have a bookstore too? *Or then again I could be wrong.*

***The amazing spurt of warm weather has tongues
once more wagging about global warming.***

I n a couple of weeks when we get walloped with snow
and the wind chills hover in the single digits no one
will make any noise about global warming. But for now
the topic of conversation is about how nice the warmth
feels. It has all the sights that you usually see on a
summer day but with some differences. I see people
wearing shorts with winter jackets on in December. I see
people wearing shorts that should not wear shorts in July.

Yesterday at the gas station I saw a man with lower
legs the size of large tree trunks. Since he was wearing
shorts you couldn't miss them. He was festooned with
tattoos of every shape color and size so as to not draw
attention to his hippo-sized legs. It wasn't working and
you couldn't help but notice him in any case. He was a
big fellow and getting bigger by the minute as he drove
away from the gas station being hand-fed French fries by
his equally large wife in good-sized handfuls. I was
pretty certain the right wheels of the car were not
touching the ground but it may have been an
optical illusion.

While I pumped gas my wife pointed at a young
lady using the coin-operated vacuum cleaner. She was in
a short winter coat with a pair of knee high boots my
parents would call mukluks. They had fur around the
tops. That would be ok except that she was also wearing
the skimpiest shorts I have seen outside of a Frederick's
of Hollywood catalogue with the word "flip" on her left
butt cheek and "chick" on the right. Watching her bend
over and vacuum was like watching a lunar eclipse if you
get my drift. The "Hot enough for you?" conversations

in mid to late December do have a somewhat surreal feeling.

The call and response includes, "This is just a tease. Yeah, wait until we get the first real snow." And so on. Just for a point of reference here for those among us who are a little sad that we won't have snow for Christmas.

At the beginning of the month in St. Louis, 19 people either froze to death or died because they had no power. Two men tried to heat their house by burning coal in a wok. They were found dead by reason of carbon monoxide poisoning.

So I am just really pleased to see a green Christmas. Every time I hear "I'll Be Home for Christmas" when it gets to the line "Please have snow," I want to strangle the singer. *Or then again I could be wrong.*

The brain police are at it again.

Those friendly folks who were revolted when Janet Jackson showed off something that they thought should have been kept under wraps are deciding what you can and cannot see on your new fangled phones. Music and video downloads are becoming quite the rage among the folks who have the new breed of cell phones. You can watch episodes of your favorite TV show, should you desire to see it on a screen the size of a slice of pepperoni, and you can set your phone to ring with the latest rap song.

But only if the phone censors have passed on it first. And boy are they being specific. When a Supreme Court justice was once asked to define pornography he replied, "I know it when I see it." Well the big guns in the cellular phone world aren't waiting around. Verizon is leading the charge with a long list of thou shall nots including: no exposed male or female genitals, no bare buttocks (that's dupas to you and me), no sex acts, no crude words or profanity (there goes most rap songs), no hate speech... whatever that means and most important no derogatory references to Verizon. Don't be thinking you can criticize them. *Uh Uh.*

They have really taken this to a new level. The guidelines include prohibiting images such as nipple shadow, see-through underwear and for men the rule that a pee pee must not appear to be "in an excited state." They have even come up with a list of 83 words you can't use on your telephone. Gee, even the FCC could only find seven. And they were really really trying!

Now let me get this straight. According to Verizon they are trying to protect customers from offensive content and protect Verizon Wireless' brand image. But you can sit down at your name any brand computer and download stuff that would make Attila the Hun gag.

That sounds like I am in favor of anything goes on your phone. Not really. But unlike TV and radio which is regulated by the FCC because the airwaves are owned by the people, a cell phone is owned by you, and according to what I know about free speech it ought to be your decision what you have or don't have on it. As long as you don't have it singing some rap song while I am next to you in the checkout line. *Or then again I could be wrong.*

The fireworks began about 3 a.m. and lasted for two hours.

A t some points it was almost a continuous stream of explosions and blinding light. My bedroom window was rattling with each explosion and sleep was just a distant memory. Mother Nature is a terrible neighbor.

Last night if a real neighbor had put on a display of fireworks like she did I would have called the cops. Who ya gonna call about the weather? I love thunder and electrical storms. Now that we have no dogs and small children in the house it's thrilling for me to watch and listen to nature's fury mauling the outside of my cozy little home.

But last night was too much even for me. Once or twice a year we get a storm like we had last night or really, early this morning. As I drove in today I heard reports of hail. It seems like we just got a buffet of weather last night.

Most times when we get a huge storm I will stand out on the porch to enjoy it. The wind in the trees and the clean smell of the rain and the symphony of the thunder is a deep pleasure that I can't experience in its fullness by staying indoors.

Last night I pulled the covers over my head. It rained hard enough that the small leak we have by the coal stove chimney pipe started dripping, so my long suffering wife had to put a cooking pot under it. After the storm finally passed we got the pleasure of listening to the drip hitting the pan. It's not a great sound. It sounds like expensive roof repairs to me. *But then again I could be wrong.*

The good news is it wasn't as bad as we feared.

T he bad news is that it's as bad as it was. As you watched the pictures and video on TV and listen to the voices on the radio you knew that we were very lucky in indeed. But try to tell to that someone in Bloomsburg where more than 25 percent of the homes are flooded out.

Mother Nature flexed her considerable muscles but for some reason spared us an Hurricane Agnes-type disaster. The images will remain with me a long time. Sad images like the little old ladies lined up with their walkers in front of them on high school bleachers. The faces of mothers clutching their children close to them with tears streaming down their cheeks as they survey the soggy mess that was only hours before a home. Funny images, like the guy with his bass boat hitched to his pickup truck, his recliner and his beer-miester in the back.

Part of my duties over the flood days found me at the press conference where they announced the forced evacuation. The County Commissioner and others who spoke were calm, cool and collected, the information was given out professionally. It made you proud to know that careful planning and what I am sure were many meetings were paying off.

I wish I could say the same for all the news media. A local TV reporter was pissed off that he had to take his personal car to the event. Imagine! A burly cameraman sweat bullets and shouted into a two-way radio trying to get his job done in what he loudly told everyone was record-breaking time. When he was offered bottled water someone muttered that he should be given a tranquilizer as well. A disgruntled newspaper writer who couldn't understand why the press conference had to be held in this room. Why couldn't we go to another bigger room where he didn't have to put up with all these cameras and microphones so close to him.

But for me the moment that I will take with me to the end of my days was this. I was using my video camera from the front seat of my car to record some of the devastation not far from where I lived. When I played it back the images clearly showed horrendous destruction that will take a long time and loads of money to fix.

But in the background over the sound of rushing water you could clearly hear the birds, tweeting and chirping their little brains out. To me it sounded like confirmation that indeed we made it through the worst of it and that life will indeed go on. *Or then again I could be wrong.*

The last few nights have been a full moon.

One night when it was clear I was up at 3 a.m. and it was bright enough to read a newspaper with. So I grabbed a copy of the *Times Leader* and perused the police blotter.

The fact that people act crazier and there is more crime during a full moon is under some dispute. In spite of the word lunacy which comes from the Latin word *luna* for moon. Some psychologists say it's a bunch of hooey. But ask any policeman or emergency room worker.

Back to the police blotter-in the past three days there have been over 60 reports printed. I don't know if that's more or less than normal but it seems like a lot. Domestic disputes, stolen vehicles, vandalism all in incredible variety. A stolen kid's bike, a ripped-off basketball hoop, a license plate taken from a car, holiday decorations stolen from a car (what holiday?). Solar lights ripped off from a front yard. Someone even liberated two air conditioners from a fire hall. Now that takes intestinal fortitude.

And a bunch of people who had more than their share of John Barleycorn. A guy arrested for throwing food and a mattress into the street. A lady who was driving on the sidewalk. A woman who was found drinking a beer in public then gave police a fake name. A 32-year-old gal arrested for exposing her breasts to passing motorists. At 9 a.m. Some things that are just plain sad.

Someone broke into a place and stole an undetermined amount of hypodermic needles. You don't need a psychologist to figure out where those will end up. A 2-year-old thrown from a car into the road, then scooped up and put back in the car which drove off. Witnesses said the car was being driven recklessly. And a man who broke into a house was found inside the residence, not his own, cooking. There are a thousand stories in the naked city under a full moon. As Warren Zevon put it. *Ahhh oooo! Or then again I could be wrong.*

*The long suffering wife pointed to the picture
on the back page of the newspaper.*

S he said, "They shouldn't be doing that. Kids look up
to them." The picture in question shows three Red
Barons celebrating after they clinched a playoff berth.
They are all firing up big old stogies the size of St.
Bernard turds and look pretty satisfied.

Now there is nothing more irritating than a former smoker crusading against the evils of tobacco. I was
a pretty good smoker in my time as a chimney, at one
point in my life up to three packs a day. I even smoked
cigars for a while but it's been years since anything
burning has been between my lips.

Cigar smoking on the surface would seem to be a
safer alternative to the cancer sticks. You don't inhale, or
at least as deeply and the rationale is that you don't smoke
quite as many cigars. Well I hate to throw water on your
fine Cubans but it's just not the case. According to the
American Cancer Society if you smoke cigars, your risk
of death from laryngeal, oral or esophageal cancers is
four to 10 times the risk compared to non-smokers.

Plus and this might be of interest to those young
healthy male ball players, a recent study found cigar
smoking, as well as cigarette smoking, is linked to
erectile dysfunction in men (the inability to achieve an
erection). Holy limp bats! Maybe the cigar
manufacturers are in cahoots with the manufactures of
Viagra to increase sales. Just a thought.

What about second hand cigar smoke?
Restaurants, bars and other public places are in the
process of banning any smoking because of it. Cigars,
again according to the American Cancer Society, have a
high concentration of nitrogen compounds. During

smoking, these compounds give off several tobacco-specific nitrosamines (TSNAs), some of the most potent human carcinogens known.

In a recent study, researchers found that the concentrations of carbon monoxide at two cigar social events in San Francisco were higher than the levels found on a busy California freeway. Had these indoor exposures lasted eight hours, they would have exceeded the National Ambient Air Quality Standards for outdoor air established by the Environmental Protection Agency.

And as to the long suffering wife's contention that "kids look up to them" you only need to look at the giveaways at the ballpark to know that youngsters are a very important market to the team. Kids fun runs and lunchbox giveaways don't really go along with cigars. Would it have made the happy ballplayers any lesser men if they had hoisted a tall, cool glass of milk instead of a stinky stogie? *Or then again I could be wrong.* Go Barons.

***It's not a daily dilemma but it happens often
enough that I wonder what is the right thing to do.***

Y ou are driving along and see a dog wandering
along the side of the road. Watching it you just
know in your heart that something is not right. The way
it moves, hesitating now and then, moving its head back
and forth. It's clear that this dog is lost, probably far from
home and needs a friend.

But, now what do you do? Just driving by and
hoping for the best seems cruel. The dog is darting in
and out of traffic and sure to get hit. Do you stop and try
to coax the critter in your car? From experience this is
easier said than done. What usually happens is the dog
gets freaked out even more, thinks you are trying to harm
it and runs away. One time the dog in question, a big
beautiful but not so smart Golden Retriever simply sat
down in the middle of the highway, right on the yellow
line and wouldn't budge.

There are a number of things to consider when
you decide to become a lost dog's savior. Is it really lost?
When you are walking after a dog by the side of the road
and it turns and runs up a driveway, the house door opens
and it runs in, you feel like a fool.

Then again you have to wonder is the dog sick or
injured? Rabies crosses your mind as does the idea that
maybe the dog has been hit already by a car and any
attempt to help will result in you getting bit.

It's a modern day dilemma that has no clear cut
answer. But I know from experience the other side. We
owned a dog once that lived to escape and run free. It was
a Siberian Husky and she was born and bred to run and
if she got loose that's just what she did. And she got free
every chance she got. She was notorious at the kennel

where we boarded her, so much so the staff began to call her Houdini.

On those occasions where I would come home and find her gone like the wind, the waiting was agony. Even when the phone would ring the first thought was someone had found her by the side of the road but too late. It never happened and she lived to be in the vet's words, "a very old woman." Still this is what makes me stop every time and try to be a friend of lost dogs. Maybe it's a bad idea but it's something I feel I owe. *Or then again I could be wrong.*

The most important phone number I have ever dialed.

This is pretty personal. That's all right. I have received quite a few emails asking me where I was the last week and half and you all deserve the answer. My 86-year-old mom had emergency surgery and was not expected to live. The critical care unit had her odds of staying on planet Earth as slim to none and slim left town.

So I hopped in the car drove to Vermont and spent the last 10 days being amazed by my miracle mom. She came out of surgery hooked up to a respirator. This means she had a tube stuck down her throat and it made it impossible for her to talk. It didn't stop her from trying to tell us stuff...and that was very frustrating for all concerned.

She was doing very well late last week so I made the choice to come back to town. It wasn't easy but I felt I had to.

Yesterday they took the tube out of her throat and I got a phone number to talk to my mom. It may seem like a small thing in the big scheme of things. But to me it meant everything. It was just a few words. But until it becomes impossible to hear your mom tell you that she loves you – you don't know how much you need to hear that.

So there you have it. I will be gone here and there over the next few weeks. Big thanks to Dave Stewart and Jack Meyer and the whole Mountain staff for putting up with my absent days and absent mind.

The next time my computer ticks me off – it's going in the dumpster.

No, I am not fabulously wealthy. But I do a LOT of work on computers. I have two on my desk at work. Sometimes three if I bring in my laptop. I have two at home. Three if you count my laptop.

At any given time one of these spawn of Satan as I refer to them will try to make me nuts. Lately however it has been taken to a higher level. This spyware and adware deal has gotten out of hand. Every day I run three programs to keep my PC from becoming a giant paperweight. And still my machines start to run slower and slower until it's so frustrating that you want to take a hammer to it. You can buy all the anti spyware you want. The demons out there are quadrupling the stuff they send you every six months.

The options when your machine turns into a turtle or freezes up all the time are: pay some one to fix it. That usually means disconnect it, drag it to the guys place and wait. Then pay $60 an hour while he figures it out. Average bill: $129. Repeat this process every six months or so and it becomes clear that option number two might begin to make sense. Drop kick the sucker out the door and head to Circuit City or Best Buy and get a cheap new one. You can find them for under $500. My livelihood depends on a fast, well-functioning computer. So for me, the prospect of spending $500 every once in a while is not overwhelming.

The only real problem is buying and getting a new computer up to speed with all your personal programs is very much like getting divorced and remarried all in one day. Someone could make a fortune here somewhere. *Or then again I could be wrong.*

The other day as I sat at a stop light,
I looked up at a small hillside.

The colors of autumn were easily visible on the slope and they were vivid indeed. Some of the trees were so bright it was almost as though they were trying to be noticed. Mother Nature's way of letting the trees say, "Look at me! Look at me!" just before there is nothing more worth looking at but bare branches.

I sat through a couple of light changes in what passes for rush hour in the Back Mountain and I had time to really inspect the vista. It was a windy day and some of the bigger trees were waving back and forth and to my caffeine-deprived, early morning mind they looked like they were sending me a message. The light changed and I moved on, pondering what the trees might have wanted me to know.

This is my favorite time of year. Crisp cool nights, bright sunny days with a spectacular clearness to the air. Someone once told me you love the time of year you are born more than others so that may be why fall has this place in my heart. Even though I hate cleaning up the mess from the leaves that brief time when they flaunt their colors and wave at me from the steep hillsides of northeast Pennsylvania gives me a great deal of joy and I cherish it.

But what message was I supposed to get from those majestic big trees waving their tops at me? Were they really waving at me? Or was it just my imagination?

The next day I was at the same spot, once more waiting in line for the same traffic light to let me through. I looked up eagerly at the trees but today the air was still and there was no motion in the tops of the tall and colorful maples or elms or whatever it was on the hillside. I drove on to work feeling a vague sense of unease, no that's too strong a word. Maybe, disappointed.

I am a big believer in signs and omens and coincidence. I have seen many times the consequences of not listening to that quiet inner voice trying to tell me something and now I wanted to know what the trees are trying to say.

The next day my gaze was lifted at the same spot and I saw a brief little wave from just one extravagantly yellow-cloaked tree. And the answer of what the trees wanted me to know came to me in an instant. *I am that I am* was the message and even this fellow who claims little or no religion looked upward and knew the trees were right. *Or then again I could be wrong.*

The other day I took a moment to rhapsodize
about the colors of the leaves and the trees
waving at me from autumn slopes.

N ow here comes reality time. I also took off from
work a bit early last Thursday to pick up those
darn leaves.

Last Thursday was a picture perfect leaf picking
up day. Crisp, clear and not so cold your hands freeze on
contact with metal objects. At the Rising Ranch we have
finally hit upon a leaf gathering system that works for us
after trying every conceivable method.

The system involves a riding lawn mower with
twin baggers for the big stuff and a self propelled walk
behind unit with bagger for those tight spots. It's tedious
work but involves no raking so it is ok by me. Can't stand
raking. So I mounted up and began the task.

As I mentioned it's mindless work so I can think
about things other than the task at hand. It's really the
only chance I get to sit and think without computer
screens, or TV screens or books or phones or long
suffering wives to distract me.

I wish I could say I think great thoughts. To be
honest most of my thinking revolves around recent
victories or defeats and how I could have done this or
that better. In my mind I try to balance the wins column
against the losses. It never seems to come out even and
you already know which way the deck is stacked.

The de-leafing of the property takes about three
hours. It's a hard enough job to earn a rest and I was glad
to just sit after the work was done. After a while though
I began to notice that my completely clean yard was
already showing some more leaves. Later that night it
rained buckets and by the next day you couldn't tell that

I had done any work at all. In a way it's sort of a metaphor for life in general. Do a good job and you get to do it again and again and again. *Or then again I could be wrong.*

***The other day we went to a show that among
other things featured recreational vehicles.***

T he dream of owing one of these has been alive in
my consciousness since I read a book called
Travels with Charley in Search of America by John
Steinbeck. It was published in 1962 when the great
author was 58. I was 10. He would die in six years. But
not before he crisscrossed the continent with the poodle
named Charlie in what we would now call a recreational
vehicle although it certainly was rather more primitive
than what we saw the other day.

Steinbeck's vehicle was a pickup truck with a
camper tossed in the cargo area. It didn't include a
bathroom, was cramped even for him and the dog. It was
poorly designed, had no insulation to speak of and was
cold in cold weather and hot in hot weather. Steinbeck
was most pleased with the fact that he could put his dirty
clothes in a suspended bucket with soap and water and
have them agitated clean by the motion of the truck as
he traveled.

As I stood in the modern RV, I wondered what he
would have thought of it. This model had everything and
the kitchen sink. Refrigerator/freezer, a full shower and
toilet, two beds, a stove and a thin screen TV set over the
dining table. Even though it was rather tiny inside it
seemed to be more spacious then you would have
thought from the outside looking in. "Everything in its
place and place for everything," as my father would
have said.

The control panels to run this home-on-wheels
were more complex than what NASA used to launch men
to the moon with switches and dials to activate air
conditioners, on board generators and for all I know a

built-in brewery. There was a crank in the ceiling that the long suffering wife was curious about. I peered at it and wasn't able to determine its function and was quickly ordered not to touch it. For all we know it might have unfolded wings and started a take-off sequence.

As we stood there admiring the cunning design, my long suffering wife's eye settled on the price tag fastened to one of the storage closets. I saw her eyes fly open wide and then she beat a hasty retreat. $71,000 and change.

Now I know it was several years ago when we bought the place we live in now. And I understand that prices on everything go up. But we are living on several acres of ground, with a house, a garage and a pool that requires yearly maintenance approaching that of a commercial airliner. And we paid several, repeat several thousand dollars less than this home-on-wheels.

I am guessing Steinbeck would have come to the same conclusion I did. Not gonna be parked in my driveway anytime soon. And he won the Nobel Prize. *Or then again I could be wrong.*

The revenge of the chimps.

I don't go to movies very often. Now I remember why. This weekend, my wife and I decided since the weather was iffy, the new *Star Wars* movie was supposed to be good and we had no NASCAR to watch on Sunday that we would go against our rule of no first week at a blockbuster movie.

We arrived at 11:30 a.m. for the 12 noon show. Sold out. The girl in the glass cage (who was speaking through a tinny mike that made her sound like a female Darth Vader) said the 12:15 p.m. show might not have two seats together. So we waited for the 12:30 p.m. show.

Well, I guess the movie was good. I will have to go see it again thanks to the family of chimps behind us in the sold-out theater. This group apparently subscribes to my new theory: The world is their toilet and they can wipe their ass on other people. Not only did they have a talkative two-year-old who would not shut up. Mommy and daddy and sister and cousin Simian and Aunt Proboscis all had to yap and yammer all through the film.

And wait there's more. The seats at the Cinemark are great. They recline. But it's not so much fun if the person behind you is kicking them and pushing on them.

Oh and did I mention the popcorn flurry? If they didn't spill one ton of popcorn I would be surprised.

Why didn't we move? Not another seat in the theater. My wife turned and hissed at them not once but twice, "Shut up." She may have as well said, "Please talk louder."

As we left the theater they were loading (in the fire lane) the family truckster up. The little two-year-old was in his baby seat. The little bastard was sound asleep. I felt like shouting "You owe me $9 and three hours of my life back." But I didn't. Monkeys have sharp teeth and powerful jaws.

The squirrels have taken up
residence in the attic again.

It's been a couple of years since the bushy tailed critters have made the space above our heads their home and I can't say I am on the welcome wagon for them.

For one thing they are noisy. I am not sure what they are doing up there but it sounds like they are setting up a rodent bowling alley. They must also have some sort of detection device that sets off an alarm when I drift off to sleep so they can make extra loud noises to wake me back up.

The last time we went through this we purchased what is known as a humane trap. It's not so much that I love the four footed squatters and wouldn't harm a whisker on their little faces as the fact that if I poison them they will undoubtedly die in the attic and stink for months.

The problem is to get to the spot where the grey interlopers live part time, we have to move almost three lifetimes' worth of attic junk out of the way. Then pile it all back again when we catch the furry fiends. Last time we did just that and exiled the squirrel far far away in a field of tall grass. But this year the long suffering wife has balked at the admittedly daunting prospect of moving all that crap and suggested we park the trap outside on the path the squirrels use to gain access to their rent free abode.

The trap was set and baited with small squares of bread with peanut butter spread on them to make it even more attractive to the bushy tailed bastards. After finding the bait gone and no squirrels I watched the trap closely and saw a chipmunk nonchalantly scurrying inside the trap and grabbing the bait, he being too light to trip the mechanism.

But with the wisdom gained from years of country living I persisted and continued feeding the chipmunk for a week or so. And then the incident.

One cold, dark and stormy morning I headed out to check and make sure the chipmunk would have his daily bread when I noticed something in the trap! Could it be we had caught Mr. Squirrel? No, but it could have been worse I guess.

Inside the trap and clearly not too happy about his predicament was the biggest opossum I have ever seen. I mean this guy's tail was as big around as a garden hose. He was too big to turn around in the trap and hissed at me from inside his prison showing far too many teeth.

I carried the trap a good distance from the house and opened the door. I didn't hang around to see him or her make good the escape but later on that day the trap was empty.

How could it have been worse? One word. Skunk. I think we will be moving junk in the attic again soon. *Or then again I could be wrong.*

Then the windshield wipers got tangled
together and snapped off, leaving me
with an even narrower field of view.

B ut I am getting ahead of myself. This past
Valentine's Day will go down in memory as the
worst snow job in northeast Pennsylvania ever and don't
forget we gave the world Joe McDade.
The storm that closed down superhighways for
days and left thousands stranded will not be soon
forgotten. I have been in some pretty bad storms in my
time but this one tops them all.

Back in the 80s, I remember a storm that occurred
while I was trying to get to New York City for a concert.
It snowed so much that they closed the New York State
Thruway and I was forced to take a room. Digging out
the next day was a feat as I had no shovel. This was back
in the days of vinyl records which I had in my car. I put
the record sleeves on my hands and used them. The trip
back was interesting. Garbage trucks had been pressed
into service with plows on the front. You haven't lived till
you have been behind five garbage trucks driving side by
side in front of you, throwing snow high in the air. As I
drove back I noticed people walking on the huge snow
banks that lined the roads. They were poking long sticks
into the snow. Then it dawned on me what they were
doing. Searching for their cars!

But that storm didn't close down the roads for two
days like our Valentine's gift. My way home is usually a 20
minute drive. I left work at 1 p.m. and arrived home just
after 5 p.m. The first leg of the journey on the interstate
was behind an 18 wheeler. The driver would move his rig
half a mile and then stop and jump out of his cab. After a
while I figured it out. He had to clean his windshield off

each time from the outside. After I finally got on the Cross Valley, it was a parking lot. Except parking lots move once in a while. Then my right hand windshield wiper stuck in the up position. The left one got tangled up and while I watched helplessly snapped off all but six inches of the blade. Didn't much matter because we weren't moving anyway.

But the worst part of the ordeal? I drink a lot of water. A four hour stay in the car with no relief sort of felt like a vasectomy without anesthesia. Have you ever tried to drive with your legs crossed? Not my idea of Valentine's Day heaven. *Or then again I could be wrong.*

There are right ways and wrong ways to fire people in this business.

I learned not to do it over the phone. I guess the most important thing about giving a person the old heave-ho is to let them vent a little. Sometimes they beg. Sometimes they cry. But if let you them do it then at least they get some of the shock, anger, and denial out of their system.

Through no fault of my own a really bad DJ had been hired to do the Saturday night oldies show. As I later got the story the fellow in question was a golf pro at the general manager's course and got him free golf or something.

Anyway this guy was a monumentally bad DJ. He talked with elaborate over pronunciation sounding as natural and friendly as a cigar store Indian. His knowledge of the music was quite good and he couldn't resist imparting it in one or two minute rambling dissertations that sounded like speech class.

And all those things could have been forgiven because after all the boss was being hooked up with free golf but for his one deadly sin. Worse than any other fault on the radio he had dead air. Not just a little here and there. But minutes of it.

There is nothing more agonizing to a program director then the sound of nothing coming out of your radio station. The longer it goes on you can just feel the twisting radio dials as they go elsewhere where the DJ is actually broadcasting something.

This guy was the all time champ at silence and it drove me to distraction. I would hot line him, call him into my office and basically read him the riot act over and over but if anything he got worse. At one point we were

175

off the air during his shift 10 times, once for two minutes. I know because I timed it, yelling at the radio and making my wife run from the room.

So I went to the GM and told him free golf or not the guy had to go. Well it seems that the silent Sam had lost his job at the golf course so I had the boss' blessing.

I ran to the phone and called the guy. Got his answering machine and without too much thought blew him out with a short message. Nothing mean, just the fact that he need not come in this Saturday night or in fact ever again. I gave the matter exactly zero thought, put in a replacement and took off for the weekend to go out of town.

I stumbled in for my air shift on Monday morning and noticed a few odd looks by the overnight guy. Finally I asked him what was on his mind. "You didn't see it?" he asked.

"What didn't I see?" I wanted to know.

He took me back out of the studio and pointed at the control room door. There was a long note from the lousy DJ full of hate and ugly character assassination on the door. It basically called into question my parentage, my ability as a program director and cheerfully predicted a dark finish to my career.

"It's been there all weekend," the overnight guy cheerfully told me.

"Well, why didn't someone take it down?" I asked.

"Because it's glued to the door!"

Sure enough the guy who couldn't play two records back to back had decoupaged this hateful note to the door with what seemed to be super glue. It took hours with a razor blade and even then you could see something had been affixed to the door. I would love to quote from this little love letter but obviously it was destroyed in the process.

It's a small business. I got to hear this character the other day on the miniscule radio station he is on. Still sounds like he has a pole up his ass, stiff as a corpse delivery. And even with all the modern technology he still has dead air.

There is a move afoot in our fair country to make restaurants post the calories contained in their offerings.

The powers that be have decided that we need to know that a Burger King meal of a triple Whopper, Coke and fries will give us 2,130 calories and we need to know it before we buy it.

I am guessing that to those folks who snarf down that kind of gut-busting chow, the calories don't mean a thing. I mean if you are in line at a fast food restaurant you already are in calorie hell so what difference does it make if you choose a Big Mac (560 calories) or a Whopper with cheese (760 calories)? Either way you are on the way to the E.R. if you eat those on a regular basis. Can you say myocardial infarction? Putting those calorie ratings on the menu boards will probably not stop anyone from ordering a heart attack on a bun, any more than the warning on the side of the cancer sticks stops a smoker from sucking down poison.

No, if they really wanted to do something useful how about posting pictures of the consequences of eating stupid. McDonald's and Burger King both have menu items with rather reasonable calorie content. The Caesar salad with chicken at both of the food giants clocks in at 220 calories, a reasonable choice for a meal. How about beside that item on the menu board instead of posting the calories you show a picture of a happy smiling young healthy couple? Make it a little sexy. Then (and you know what's coming here don't you?) next to the really high calorie items on the menu put a picture of a frowning angry fat person. A single angry frowning fat person. The more calories, the fatter the person you post.

Don't stop there. On the wrapper put a picture of an extra large sized person in skimpy shorts or a tank top with rolls of fat squeezing out. Make them look like they don't enjoy life. The message should be, *eat this and be like me.* Angry and not sexy. And single. Definitely single with no love life.

Come to think of it maybe you could deter smokers the same way. Instead of that useless warning on the smokes why not a picture of a lung riddled with cancer? Or a coffin with loads of flowers around it. You get the drift. Of course then we would have to put pictures of car wrecks on beer bottles. Truth in advertising? It'll never happen. *Or then again I could be wrong.*

There is something soothing about a routine.

For the past few years my long suffering wife and I have made the rounds of area flea markets, yard sales and the like. This past month for reasons I am not really going to go into here, we have not had the time or the inclination. But in an effort to put our lives back on track we resumed the routine this past weekend.

We make a circuit, the Mrs. and me. The 8th and 6th Streets flea market. The Garden Drive Inn. Ely Street. Sometimes we pack in a full day down the line at Saylorsburg.

But nothing can quite compare with the sights, smells, sounds and experience of a trip to Lackawanna County and the Circle Drive-In and then up the Scranton Carbondale to the former Sugerman's. Yesterday the Circle Drive-In was rockin'! The joint was jumpin' to say the least.

Almost as soon as you enter your senses are assaulted. It's really what I would imagine a Third World bazaar might have been in the days of the Bible. Except of course they wouldn't have had light bulbs on sale. Stacks and crates and boxes full of every type of light bulb you can imagine. Boxes covered in dust and yellowed from age. I overheard one person remark, "Edison must have made those light bulbs they be so old."

It's cheap entertainment. Parking is 50 cents at the Circle. You can hear a multitude of tongues being wagged in a United Nations of languages. Hispanic accents haggling with Asian vendors over used tools that I couldn't identify if you hit me over the head with them.

And the things you see…. A huge parrot screeching at full volume cowers a German Shepherd dog. A girl with faded pink hair walks by and I wonder about the thought process there. A full display of really gruesome skulls with red railroad spikes driven through them brings a laugh from my wife but the Goth chick with way too many piercings on her face looks them over with a serious eye. A man with an indescribable collection of ….stuff sits on an overturned Herrs potato chip barrel and beseeches us to buy something, anything. He will sell us the vest he is wearing off his back. No sale. The man carrying the parrot buys a street sign with metal pole attached for Lick Road. If you folks on Lick Road were wondering what happened to the sign, there's your sign.

Up the road to Sugerman's, the former Polish Disneyland, as I have heard it called. The entire store is filled with small vendors, ranging from rather completely stocked drug stores, some items expired buyer beware, to huge mountains of well…junk. Old switch plates. Amputated plugs from electrical appliances. Piles of moldering LPs. And for those of you who want to keep up on the latest technology a sign offering a used VZR. I guess it's sort of like a VCR but further down the alphabet.

It's just another weekend at the flea market. And I am thankful beyond words for it. *Or then again I could be wrong.*

There must be a parallel universe where
people who write letters to the editor live.

I wonder what color the sky is there. The other day the tabloid that calls itself a newspaper (don't worry, it'll grow up to be a real full size newspaper someday) printed a letter from someone who we call Rick because that's his name.

Rick, who lives in Hanover Township was bitching because in his opinion as a deer hunter, *dere ain't anuff does.* Or what Rick really said was there aren't any deer anymore.

Well Rick, I hate to be a disagreeable guy but I have to respectfully beg to differ. Join me on my travels around the Dallas, Pennsylvania area some time, Rick, and I will show you so many deer you will be flabbergasted.

Rick's letter accuses the state game commission of mishandling the deer herd. Tell it to my shrubbery, Ricky. The thing is I don't dislike deer, but when they are in my backyard munching on stuff I planted to make the hacienda look pretty, I get a little perturbed.

And driving in the early morning hours is like playing dodge ball with Bambi and her extended family. The other day I had to stop while a herd, and I mean fewer than 20 but more than a dozen deer decided to cross the road in front of me. This is a spot less than a mile from a gas station, hoagie shop and a bank. And this is not a one time occurrence.

Back when I first moved here from New England I was amazed at seeing deer from my car, something we never did in Vermont. I would stop and watch the little critters in open mouthed wonder, squealing with excitement. Now the only squeal I hear is from my brakes as I try not to catapult the creatures off my bumper.

Wait a minute, I think I have spotted Rick's problem. In his letter he talks about hunting in the woods and coming home with no deer. Ricky, Ricky, Ricky – I have solved your problem. Just buy a new big expensive SUV. Drive it too fast on any road in the Back Mountain and you will collect your deer pretty fast, along with some expensive body work on the land yacht. *Or then again I could be wrong.*

Things to be thankful for.

S pring version. Here with a short list of what I like about May and early June. Your mileage may vary. Daffodils. I love the ones with the white centers. Runner up in the flower category. Tulips. When someone has taken the time to plant a lot of tulips in various colors they should be applauded.

Baby bunnies. If you don't believe in a higher power then you have never watched a bunny the size of a walnut munching dandelion stems in the back yard. Runner up in the animal category. Fawns. When they still have spots. Too bad they grow up to be road kill.

A warm but not hot sunny day. In springtime before the bugs are out in force. A few minutes in the sun watching the clouds and listening to the birds. Runner up in the time wasted category? There is no runner up.

Bird songs. Best in the pre-dawn to dawn hours. Runner up in the bird song category? Just before nightfall. At either time the joyous chorus can do a lot to sooth the stress that listening to the noise other humans make provides.

The return of the flea markets. A few hours poking through piles of stuff, mostly junk but always interesting if not for any actual value but for the almost unbelievable variety of what people think other people might buy. Runner up. The variety of festivals. From art to cherry trees you can enjoy it on a warm spring day in our area. And hardly a weekend goes by without at least one.

That first day after a long winter where you can go without a coat in the morning. It's like you forget what it's like to feel the air on your arms. Runner up. Putting the storm windows up and the screens down. Letting the air and the bird songs in again.

The first hummingbird at the feeder. Proof God has a sense of humor. Runner up. The squirrels return and chase each other around again. I know they must be around in winter but these days they perform better acrobatics than anything you can see in the circus.

The shovels are packed away and the lawn mower is out. Call me crazy but even though cutting the grass is a pain, equal time spent mowing the lawn or shoveling snow is not equal time. Rare is the day spent behind the lawn mower in a parka with hat and mittens.

So it's spring time in northeast Pennsylvania. The bare trees are lush with greenery, the tax refund check is already spent and all is right with the world. *Or then again I could be wrong.*

This all began with a botched root canal.

Ten years ago I had a dentist who was in training to be a butcher. Actually I think he ended up in the travel industry. I hope that he doesn't ever fly a plane. Anyway this miserable excuse for a dentist did several root canals on me and none of them have ever been right. I suffered with them for a long time but a couple of weeks ago one became real painful.

So off I went to my dentist who promptly referred me to an oral surgeon. Now I have no problem with the oral surgeon. He did make a small mistake but fixed it right away and was very apologetic about it. And his assistant in the procedure could not have nicer or more professional.

But the girls in the front office. There are names I have heard women called that I can't say here. These lovely ladies deserve all of them.

My first greeting at the window was a five minute wait while the three behind the glass finished their blatantly personal conversation. I found out more about their lives than I really wanted to know. Finally I get some attention. "What?" was the attention. I was a little taken aback but I managed to get out my name. "Ok, siddown." I saddown.

And while I was waiting I saw the most amazing amount of rudeness and vile behavior I have seen in my life. And don't forget I have an ex-wife and I have been to domestic relations. These ladies were inexcusably rude to everyone.

One girl came to the window. Asked and had answered a question. Then as she walked away the behind the glass gang made fun of her. She went back to the window and said, "I heard that and I hope someday you get treated like you just treated me." *Whew.* Just another day at the beach.

I discovered the dentist's minor mistake a few days later and called him at night to see what I should do. He told me to come in the next day first thing.

I resented the fact that when I stood at the window that morning that I still had to wait while the three magpies had their little chat. Finally my turn. "What?"

I said my name.

"Well..you don't have a appointment."

"No, but the dentist wants to see me."

"Well, siddown."

"No," I said.

"What?" the shocked lady exclaimed.

"The dentist will see me now," I said.

"I'm afraid it doesn't work like that," she snapped at me.

Just then the dentist came around the corner and saved us all from an unpleasant exchange.

You know it costs nothing to be nice. And it makes the whole experience of living so much better. I suspect those three had better upbringing than they were displaying. But somewhere along the way it all got lost. *Or then again I could be wrong.*

This is a dirty subject but I have to talk about it.

C lear small children form the room. On second thought, bring them in the room because they need to hear this most of all. Maybe if they get trained at an early age this dirty subject won't be something we ever need to talk about.

The question is….why don't people flush? I can understand a certain environmental consciousness that has to do with saving water and all that. But not flushing? *Pullease.* It's bad enough to face the bowl and discover the water quite yellow from previous use. But to get a look at a pile of number two, flagged with mounds of T.P. is downright revolting.

What is the problem here? You do your business. You WIPE your business and then you flush. Even feeble old ladies have the strength to work the flush handle. Why can't the muscle-bound jarhead guys at my gym do the same?

The toilet at the gym has one of those super-charged flushing actions. It forces air or something along with the water at high pressure. I mean this thing flushes. You could put a watermelon down it.

So why this morning it was filled to the brim with you know what is truly beyond me. I blame the cretin who unplugged my treadmill a while ago and then smirked at me. He looks like the type who thinks the world is his toilet.

I guess Freud would say that those who don't flush are showing the world that they can make doo doo and are darn proud of it. Never grew out of the anal retentive stage.

And don't get me started about urinals. Let's just say that yellow doesn't mellow when it sits. It's the small things that make civilization great or awful I think. And unflushed toilets are just another sign post on the slippery slope to the warm place.

This is going to sound a bit like I am a music snob.

I have been accused of this before and it's really not the truth but you may take it anyway you wish. The summer concert season is starting to get filled up. Loads of great shows close by and I am very glad that we get our share of the tours here in good old northeast Pennsylvania.

I must admit, however I probably won't go to that many shows. Sure, if we do a bus trip I will go along and probably enjoy the hell out of it, but to tell the truth..and here's where the snob part comes in...I have seen most everybody I really wanted to in my life as a music guy and some of my heroes. Well I don't think they can enhance my already great memories. Like what kind of memories?

Well my concert experiences may be somewhat different from the perspective that I get to see the backstage antics and usually have access to places that a lot of people don't. That said let me give you a few highlights of my concert going experiences.

I saw The Call when they were at Lackawanna County Stadium. It was a shitty day, rainy and cold. The crowd was very small and the band played their axes off! It was an emotional high for me and I almost felt a religious conversion. We met them (The Call) afterward and they couldn't have been nicer. That ranks near the top 10.

I saw Paul McCartney in the 90s. His show was amazing and brought tears to my eyes. He refused any backstage and in a way I was glad. It's one of the few times I just went to a concert and was enthralled.

I saw Steve Miller in the 70s and the show was great. We met him at a backstage buffet. He was forcing shrimp into his mouth three at a time and shook hands with me leaving cocktail sauce on me. When he said, "Hi," he sprayed me with shrimp. A few years later I saw him again and he had gained like 100 pounds!

A George Thorogood show at the Kirby (and I love George) was preceded by a meet & greet for a small number of fans. His road manager came out beforehand and said (and he was yelling) "Don't be TOUCHING George! Don't be trying to hug or kiss him or take his clothes off. Keep your distance. Don't speak to him unless he speaks to you!"

George came in and ordered shots for everyone from the mini bar. He lined them up on the bar and said, "Come on everybody, have a drink on me!" No one moved. We were all terrified. George looked confused, then left.

A Rick Springfield show at the Armory in the early 80s was where I met my wife. He was a soap star and had some big records. For some reason, I was under the stage, right under where he was standing when he came out. I could see the crowd, almost 100 percent female and I physically FELT the lust projecting from them to a spot above my head where Rick was. It was like a laser beam!

Later on that night I saw a gal with a wedding dress in plastic on a hanger. She was, um how to put this, "riding" a railing with the dress over her shoulder, eyes shut moving back and forth. So how could I build on memories like that?

This is such a glamorous job.

T his radio deal. Well it is sort of cushy now. The
heaviest lifting I have to do is CDs and usually
only a few at a time.

Radio in the early years wasn't quite so
glamorous. The technology in the time when I started
out in the business was not nearly as sophisticated as it is
now and radio station owners, at least in the *ahem*, small
towns I was working in were terminally cheap. Back in
those days we used actual turntables, remember those,
kids? Big black vinyl records.

Anyway one place I worked was on top of a
mountain. The transmitter was actually housed right in
the control room, with the antenna right outside the back
door. Must be why I had several square babies, all that
radiation.....the management discovered with the big old
transmitter right there in the building that they could
heat the joint in the cold New England winter with the
hot air the transmitter produced. Summers they just let
us sweat.

What they didn't take into account was that
station went off the air at midnight, transmitter turned
off and no heat. The first real cold snap when our hero
arrived the next morning to start the morning show it
was below freezing in the control room. Icicles had
formed on the microphone. Real tough to be bright and
cheerful with your teeth chattering. But the worst part?
The turntables were cold and ran really slow. So all the
music sounded like Lurch from the *Addams Family*.

The reason I am tripping down memory lane here
is that we had a bad day at the office yesterday. Our email
and internet were down all day and most of the people
here were genuinely distressed. No internet? How can

we possibly do our jobs? I wasn't concerned at all. It's a simple matter of perspective. When you've had to do radio with an inch of frost on the control board, you can pretty much handle anything. *Or then again I could be wrong.*

This really shouldn't be an issue, but it is.

The lesson was taught in the home, in kindergarten and all through grade school. And yet it's estimated that over 75 percent of men (I don't know about women) don't do it. They don't wash their hands after peeing. Some don't even visit the sink after going number two which is really disturbing.

There are some interesting arguments about why not to wash your hands after peeing. Some make the claim, which is true, that urine is sterile when it leaves the bladder. While this is true, the fact that is really is more to the point, would you want to drink your own pee?

Some claim they don't get any on their hands. But those same guys neglect to think about the splash factor. When you stand at the urinal you spray. Spraying makes some of the pee into aerosol form which then drifts onto your hands. Please forgive me if I don't want to shake hands with you after that mini-shower from your urethra.

I understand why sometimes it's a little tough to wash your hands in some men's rooms I have been in. A dirty sink can deter your desire to wash up as will the lack of soap or worse yet the dreaded warm air dryer in place of paper towels.

That damn air hand dryer probably contributes more to the spread of disease than any paper towel in spite of the smug claim on its face plate that it's designed to prevent just that. First of all the stupid things don't work. You are left with damp hands and those are like magnets for germs which you will come into contact just by using the door handle on the bathroom. Second fact, there is little to no chance that you will get a disease from someone else using a towel in the bathroom. Unless you rub said towel in your eyes and all over your body, how could you? The only problem you are preventing is the prospect of unemployment for the evil people who make and sell the hot air hand dryers.

My solution as usual will solve both problems. Pass tough legislation to ban all hot air hand dryers. Take all the hot air hand dryer company employees, salesmen and maintenance guys and put them to work in bathrooms across the land. Train them to insist on hand washing after every elimination and pay them handsomely. The money for their paychecks could come from the savings in electricity from the now outlawed hand dryers and from a grateful world that spends less time sick from germs. Problems solved. *Or then again I could be wrong.*

Today I will say the three scariest words ever spoken in the house.

F irst let me rant a bit. I have been a home owner for more years than I care to admit. It's a joy and a curse all rolled into one thing. The hardest part? Home maintenance. And the hardest part of the upkeep? Getting someone to show up and fix something.

Sometimes even getting a return phone call is impossible. I don't know if this is peculiar to northeast Pennsylvania or not. I do know that it's real common here. Pick up the newspaper and call a few home repair people. These are guys who are advertising to find work.

I did this a while ago to offer a pretty good amount of work. Out of eight guys I called three returned calls. One actually showed up to look at the job. He ended up doing it...slowly. But that's another story.

The three scariest words? The toilet's leaking! That was my wake up call yesterday morning at 5:30 a.m. Something in the tank had gone horribly wrong. Water was cascading out all over the bathroom floor.

Now I am NOT a home handyman by any stretch of the imagination. I have a unique ability to make a simple job hard and usually ruin something in the process. So I have developed a special skill when it comes to fix-it-now emergencies. I pick up the phone and dial.

After shutting off the water...and I must add that this is the first time that when I twisted the shut-off knob under the toilet tank that it didn't break off in my hand.

I picked up the phone. When you call a plumber who advertises 24 hour service you get an answering service. I gotta figure the plumber doesn't sit by the phone waiting for it to ring at 5:30 a.m. The guy at the answering service sounded pretty annoyed at me, why I don't know. "Did I want someone to call during normal business hours or right now?"

"Right now would be good," I said.

Heavy sigh from the service. "Oh, all right," he muttered.

An hour and a half later I called back, and this time got the owner. I have to say that if you need plumbing in a hurry done professionally and without an attitude, here is a tip – R N. Fitch in Dallas, Pennsylvania at 570-675-0646.

Oh the leak – a bolt on the bottom of the tank had rusted away. And small consolation – it didn't choose last week to do this while I was out of town.

Today is Veterans Day.

At the risk of sounding like a bad country and western song my daddy was a vet. He nearly lost his leg in some Asian rim crap hole. He and his generation never ever talked about the war. I saw my father in the company of men that I knew he served in the Marine Corps with and never so much as heard a war reference, never mind a war story. Even with alcohol fueling the get together.

One time when I was 12 or 13-years-old I spent a few hours trying to get him to talk about it into a tape recorder for some sort of school project. My dad was a real smart man and it took him a very short time to bore me to tears with a highly philosophical ramble that was not what I expected or wanted. He did not want to set back my project by saying no but he sure wasn't going to give me the gory details. No offense dad, but I don't know if it was the right way to handle it.

It kindled in me (and I think in many of my generation) a curiosity in what the big secret was. It lead me to watch many, many war movies and read every book I could get my hands on about the subject. But I wonder this. If I had been the right age to go to Vietnam (and I narrowly missed that dubious honor) would I have gone? Would the mystery of what war was, what it would be like to have my war, been a strong enough draw to put me in harm's way? Secrets are very motivating, especially to young guys. I will never know. And now after watching Hollywood render war with *Apocalypse Now*, *Full Metal Jacket* and the *Deer Hunter*, I am glad I didn't go over there.

The code of silence that surrounds modern warfare is not what it was in my dad's time. We see more on TV shows that masquerade as entertainment then we used to see on the six o'clock news. I think that's probably a good thing. Anything to keep 19-year-olds out of body bags is ok with me.

This, by the way has nothing to do with being patriotic. I love this country, I respect what vets did to keep it the way I love it. And when the cause it right and just I think we should do what we have to defend our very special way of life. But our country do or die? I don't think even my father would buy that one.

We cut the grass for the first time
this year over the weekend.

I would like to meet the guy who decided that we have to do this. Why is it that in order to be judged a civilized neighbor you must have the grass in your yard trimmed regularly to an inch or so? But trim we must. So I spent the better part of my Saturday morning while I was waiting for the dew to dry on my lawn firing up and testing out the devices I would need to do the deed. Riding lawn tractor, self propelled lawn mower and weed whacker.

The first project is to get all these devices started. The proper storage method for anything powered by a gasoline engine is to drain the fuel completely out, put some stuff in the tank that is supposed to keep the lines clear and carefully store the item in a cool dry environment. Of course I do none of this stuff so I spend a long time trying to start the engines each spring.

Last year at the end of the season I treated myself to a new weed whacker. The old one was getting cranky about starting and there were some issues with the gizmo that feeds the line out. Issues like it wasn't working.

But the old memory isn't what is used to be. So I wasted about an hour getting the old weed whacker to run. This involved approximately 1,000 pulls on the starter rope. My right arm is so sore right now that even typing is making the muscles cry out in pain. After the 1,001 pull on the starter rope, I did what every calm, cool, and collected mature home owner would do. I threw the weed whacker at the back wall of the garage.

Which as it turns out was a stroke of genius because it bounced and landed on top of the new weed whacker which started on the second pull. In the process of unearthing all the current lawn mowing implements, I found an old lawn mower that to put it mildly had seen better days. Although it started ok, the self propelled mechanism had long since given up and it was much too heavy to push. I also discovered my old mountain bike. By old, I mean I haven't ridden it in 20 years. Tires were flat, it had more rust then frame and the seat was moldy.

Both of these items went to end of the driveway with a sign that said, "Free." The mower was gone in an hour, the bike in about three. My biggest fear. That they will reappear in the night. *Or then again I could be wrong.*

We knew were in trouble when the two truckloads of huskies passed us.

L et me back up a bit here. My brother was having a milestone birthday last week. So as to protect his dignity I will not mention that it was his 60th. Let's just say he is older than Father Time and leave it at that.

My brother lives in the area of our country that some people refer to by the quaint term "Vermont." My long suffering wife calls it "*Brr*-mont" but she has never met a snow drift she liked. I grew up in the Green Mountain State so I have more affection for the place than she does. You have to love a place where the definition of summer goes: Summer? Oh, we swim on that day.

We struck out for Vermont on a clear and sunny day to try and be part of a surprise party for my much older brother. It's funny how much older he has gotten. I have remained at about the same age while he just keeps piling on the years. I think it has something to do with Einstein's Theory of Blood Relations.

As we drove along the ominous weather reports began. The radio said things like: four feet of snow, five feet, 100 inches. Snow drifts higher than 10-story buildings. National Guard called out. State of emergency declared.

My long suffering wife quietly asked, "That's not where we are going, is it?"

"Of course not," I confidently replied, wishing I was sure about our route north.

It was at this point that I noticed the two large trucks behind us. It looked like they had dog sleds on top. As they passed we could see not only the sleds but little cages with Husky-type dogs inside. I don't believe in omens but this seemed like a bad sign.

As it turned out we completely avoided any snow. The only things we had to contend with were the bitter cold (at times the wind-chill in the Green Mountain State was absolute zero, the temperature that all life stops) and the directions to my brother's house deep in the Vermont woods. I should have known we were in trouble when we got to the part about the bridge being closed because they don't plow it.

By the way the party was a huge success. By all appearances my elder brother was surprised by the huge gathering in his house deep in the Vermont woods. I think grabbing his chest and falling down was a good sign don't you? *But then again I could be wrong.*

Well it's finally really spring.

I got my little convertible out and took it for a bunch of rides over the past few days. It's amazing what you see from that perspective. You see, my little "mid-life crisis" car is a 1974 MGB. It's about the size (and power) of a good sized riding lawn mower. Except it's only about four inches off the ground. From that perspective with the top down you get a whole new experience in driving.

I also am firmly convinced that lunacy follows me on the highways. Or precedes me. I got off I-81 the other day with a small black sedan in front of me. It looked sorta funny, like it was, I dunno, listing to the right. I could (from my four inches off the ground perspective) see something flapping on the right hand front tire. I got over to the side enough so I could check it out. Yup, the right front looked like a NASCAR blowout. Pieces of tire flapping the fender and flying off. The driver put the four ways on by the time he got to the light across from the Wyoming Valley Mall.

Good, I thought. At least he's aware of the problem. His passenger tossed a smoke out the window. Well at least they weren't in a blind panic. We proceeded in "O.J." slow motion down the road. There's a tire place just after the Taco Bell. Surely he will pull in and get it looked at. Nope, cruised right on by. Took a turn and then headed into Wilkes-Barre on the main drag. I lost him when I turned to go to Public Square. For all I know he might still be driving.

I had to pick up tickets at the F.M. Kirby so I parked in the bus stop. I know, bad on me but I knew it would only be a minute. And it was just about that when I got back in my fine British sports car. Which refused to start. Just gave me an apologetic "click." It's done this before. But not with buses waiting behind me. Blowing their horns. And people all around. Close. I said a really sincere prayer and the thing fired. I was never so relieved in my life except for the time that...well that's another story.

I don't want you to think that I am rolling in the dough. I bought my little heartbreaker on eBay for a couple of thousand. I have put a few bucks into it but it's more of a labor of love than anything else.

I have had all sorts of interesting breakdowns though. Like the first night. I started it in the garage and backed it out and noticed – oil, everywhere. Like a lot of oil. Like all the oil in the engine, now staining the garage floor and the driveway. A tow to the MG repair man found no good reason for this...just a loose oil filter!

Then there was the first LONG ride in the country with my not-so-thrilled wife. The car is LOUD! And it rides...not so smooth. But to give her credit she puts up with it. In the middle of nowhere...the throttle cable snapped. I had NO tools. Nothing. With safety pins and sewing thread from my wife's purse, I fixed it enough to get us home. Now I carry spare parts and loads of tools. But every ride is an adventure. Just ask my wife.

Whoever said that a man's home is his castle hasn't been in Wilkes-Barre lately.

I t seems that that well worn cliche doesn't apply any more, at least to the 15 or 20 feet in front of his castle. It's become obvious that contrary to popular belief you don't own the parking space in front of your house, at least according to the Wilkes-Barre police.

There have been numerous tiffs recently over the question of who parks where and at least one of them has involved gun play. Gun play over a parking space? My how our little town is growing. The worse confrontations used to be in winter when someone would clean the space in front of their humble home and then return to find someone had usurped their hard effort. I would be a little ticked off too. Maybe not mad enough to put someone in the hospital which happened last month on Poplar Street where a parking space skirmish ended in a broken nose and leg but I would have mad.

Now, I live out in the country so parking spaces are the least of my worries. We are more concerned with deer eating the shrubbery and marauding bears. But I used to live in a row house in the downtown Wilkes-Barre area. And thankfully I had no problem with always having the parking space in front of my shotgun shack open. Because I had a secret weapon.

His name was Decker. I was never sure if that was his first or last name. Truth be told I never understood more than a few words he said. And he really didn't say much. Decker was my next door neighbor. Built along the lines of a fireplug, Decker had a voice like someone had thrown marbles in a cement mixer. I met him when I knocked on his door once to ask him if he wouldn't mind letting the cable man in my house while I was at work.

"No problem," Decker replied and I gave him a few bucks for his trouble. After that Decker was my parking space guardian angel.

He apparently didn't work so he would clean snow from my space, sweep in front of my house and most importantly chase people away from parking in my spot. All for a few bucks here and there.

I never saw any confrontations but I can't imagine anyone arguing with Decker. Decker may have been short but he had Popeye arms and a certain menace in his demeanor. Decker could obviously kick some dupa.

So I think the problem of parking spots in downtown Wilkes-Barre could be easily solved. Just get a bunch of rent-a-deckers and everything will work out fine. *But then again I could be wrong.*

Why is it that some guys insist on calling you nicknames?

I see the wisdom in addressing someone you see everyday in some way but I am sorry to say that because you are in line in front of me at the Convenient Mart two or three times a week doesn't make me your "pal," your "buddy" or even give you the right to call me "big guy." I don't know you. If I did I would greet you by your name and I assume you would too. So the "pal" stuff is just because you don't know my name, right? I would prefer almost anything else. "Hey, you" would be preferably to the "buddy" routine.

I guess the problem stems from the incident at the flea market in Saylorsburg a few weeks back. The Blue Ridge Flea Market is a pretty intense experience, not for the faint of heart. It's more than 25 acres of everything under the sun and some things and people that would be better left in darkness.

The parking lot for this giant flea market is a joke. Pitifully small, dusty and carved out of a field with boulders and large trees left in the way, it's a challenge to find a space and like the pot of gold at end of the rainbow when you get one near the action.

The day in question after circling the parking lot 25 times and nearly getting sideswiped or rear-ended a dozen times a space appeared right in front of the booths. It seemed too good to be true and as it turns out it was.

As I walked away from the car (my long suffering wife was far ahead of me having departed for the action like a sprinter) a huge guy stood in front of me and said, "Hey pal, that's my space. You'll have to move."

I looked back at the space and try as I might I couldn't see a reserved sign, an orange cone or a sawhorse marking his territory. I told him this and his reply was, "Hey, buddy I been here 15 years and that's my space."

I remarked that it was not my problem and began to walk away. He called me a name, not so much under his breath. A name that rhymes with grassmole if you get my drift.

I turned and asked him to repeat it and his quick retort was, "You heard what I said, pal."

Rather then fight to the death over a parking space at a flea market I just said, "I'm not your pal and I'm not moving."

Of course I spent the whole day looking over at the spot praying that my car wouldn't be in flames. *But then again I could be wrong.*

Why is it?

T he other day it was National Whine Day at work. I don't know if it was the full moon or what but every single person came to me whinnying with some big problem that I was supposed to make all better. I thought maybe I deserved to whine a little so here you go.

Why is it that the same motion detector lights that won't turn on in the dark when I am carrying the groceries in a blinding rainstorm will turn on when the wind blows...and stay on all night?

Why is it that when the store has double doors, one – and it's the one I always pick – is locked?

Why is it that when the self-propelled lawn mower runs out of gas it's at the farthest point from the gas can?

Why do people tailgate more the lower the speed limit is?

Why is it when you are really hungry and order soup so it comes fast, that's the only thing they don't bring? Why is it always on the bill?

Why when there are an equal number of lines at the checkout and they are equally filled do I always pick the one that moves the slowest?

Why do childproof caps on my medicine make me spill all the pills on the floor every time I open the bottle?

Why does the power go out just before I save my work on the computer?

Why does all that spam get through my email but that important email from the boss goes directly to the spam file?

Why do cars, dental work and prescription glasses always break when you are on vacation?

Why is it when you haven't shaved or combed your hair for three days and run to the store for the newspaper you meet everyone you know?

Why does the printer run out of black ink in the middle of a ten page report?

Why do you always run out of toilet paper with nobody else in the house after Mexican food?

Why does the water change temperature in the shower after you have soap in your eyes so you can't find the faucets?

Why does the guy ahead of me in the drive through have to be ordering for the whole office?

Why is it that the neighbor's dog is constipated in his yard but has no problem in mine?

Why is it when everyone else in the restaurant is laughing and joking with their waitress I get the one who hates her job and doesn't like me much either?

There – now I feel better. *Or then again I could be wrong.*

With all due apologies to the hundreds of restaurants in the area that serve buffets – I can't stomach it.

Oh yes, I am guilty of the occasional trip to the salad bar. But those endless mazes of hot and cold buffets are too much for me in so many ways.

First of all the whole concept is a little bit on the unappetizing side. Food is supposed to come out the oven or pot and onto my plate. Not sit like a car in a showroom waiting for someone to pick it. And when you do choose something that looks appetizing doesn't it always seem like it doesn't taste as good as it looked?

A buffet is all you can eat. I have been to some buffet restaurants that have some regular customers who definitely have had all they can eat and all you and I and some Third World nations could eat too. Now I am not a skinny guy so I can't say too much here but some of these buffet gals and guys need to show a little restraint at the restaurant. And a little mercy to their stretch waistbands, if you get my drift.

Now here's my major maladjustment when it comes to buffets. Other people. Other people who I don't know are in close proximity to my chow. These are folks who for all I know clean sewers for a living. Or who don't wash their hands after going number two. While they don't, I hope, actually touch the food they certainly touch the serving utensils and then I get to touch them by proxy. *Ewww.* Even the best buffet is set up so you have to reach over some of the offerings to get to the steaming pile of stuff you want. Hope nothing shakes loose from someone's sleeve.

And then there's the kids at buffets. Don't get me started. I once saw a tiny urchin pile his already used plate with some food, change his mind and PUT IT

BACK! And when I spoke to the little creep about this his mother yelled at me! "He's been taught not to waste food," she shouted at me. Yeah, right.

Do you know what they call those little awnings over buffets? Sneeze guards. Think about that for a moment. The designers of the buffet concept actually expect the food will be protected from sneezing buffet-goers the size of water buffalos by that contraption?

One popular buffet style restaurant in the Back Mountain that is now a pile of dirt in an empty lot, lost my business early on. It was set up so the buffet line ran along the kitchen and had one way sliding glass mirrors so the cooking and serving staff could see the buffet and replenish it and you couldn't see them.

Except for some reason I could see them. They were looking at the customers, making faces at them and generally doing rude and obscene things behind the scenes. Pretending to pick your nose and then handling food has never seemed funny to me. I never went back.

I'm not even going to mention my sneaking suspicion about some buffets. I will just say one word and let you figure out the rest. Recycling. *Or then again I could be wrong.*

*With the years and tears piling up on me
and the other members of my generation
sometimes you have to worry about what
Nancy Regan called "the long goodbye."*

I t seems to me anyway that the threat of living out the golden years with dementia is very scary. So it was with a little trepidation that I saw an article in *USA Today* the other day listing five signs of impending Alzheimer's. As I read through the list I began to get that *uh-oh* feeling. Of course like medical school students who think they get every disease they study it could just be false warning signs but still.

Here they are. Sign # 1: Forgetting recently learned information. Yup. That would be me. I can't remember a phone number from the time I read it in the phone book till the time I begin to dial it. Tell me your name? I won't know it by the time we stop shaking hands.

Sign # 2: It is difficult to complete everyday tasks, such as dialing the phone. See Sign # 1. *Uh oh.*

Sign # 3: Simple words such as toothbrush or car cannot be recalled. The long suffering wife and I make a game out of this. Well, I do anyway. It goes something like this. "Hand me the pickle sauce."

"You mean the ketchup?"

"Yeah that's what I said."

I laugh glad that she has played another round of name that thing but sometimes it's not a joke. Double *uh-oh.*

Sign #4: Frequently placing things in odd places such as putting a shoe in the refrigerator. *Phew!* I am clear on that one at least. Now how DID the remote control get in the microwave?

And finally sign #5: Rapid mood changes for no apparent reason. Well at least I am clear on that one. I mean don't get me wrong I can go from zero to tantrum in less time than it takes to blink but it's always for a GOOD reason. Like the computer loses one of my rants. Or I stub my toe. Or a cloud covers the sun. Or...*uh oh. Or then again I could be wrong.*

***It's the holiday season and whoop di do hickory
dock, don't forget to have your gun cocked –
they'll be ripping off your safe tonight.***

There is nothing funny about the recent robbery of an 85-year-old Nanticoke, Pennsylvania resident. John Miller had his house busted into and the two large black men took $1,600 in cash from his safe, roughing him up a bit in the process. The money, John says was earmarked for Christmas presents and now his grandkids will have nothing for the holiday.

What is disturbing about this story is that John has said that he usually only opens his door with a loaded gun in his hand. He didn't this time because, well it's the holiday season and he expected it to be friends or family not two big men with larceny in their heart.

But back to this idea of answering your door with a gun. Is this what it's come to in this area? I used to take great pride in telling folks from out of town that I live in Mayberry RFD. By that I mean this place is safe, secure and you can leave your door unlocked at night. I stopped doing that a while ago and now I wonder if John has the right idea.

The local crime rate continues to skyrocket. Not to be cynical about it but it's pretty obvious that big men are coming from out of town, New York and Philly probably to knock over the dumb hicks in the countryside of northeast Pennsylvania. I have heard that the type of person who forced John to open his safe and dispense his hard- earned Christmas booty refer to our convenience stores as ATM machines. Just ripe for the picking. And the number of purses snatched from the shoulders of trusting little old ladies in mall parking lots is something that should give us all pause.

I hope that the cops catch the two men who robbed John. He called them "bastards" in a newspaper article and he is not wrong. John also said he wished he did have his gun at door that fateful night. He would have shot those bastards dead, he says.

I am not too thrilled with the idea of 85-year-old men answering their doors with guns at the ready. But I am less in favor of our area becoming more like a war zone than Mayberry RFD.

Isn't there a way to fix this? Or are we doomed to become just like the big cities. I stand alert on the slippery slope to hell, just pointing at the sign posts. *Or then again I could be wrong.*

You can learn all sorts of fascinating things by reading the letters to the editor in newspapers.

The other day the headline read, "Start your day with two shots of whiskey." Naturally, I was intrigued. It seems that Jake from Edwardsville has suggested to a number of and I quote here, "leading research facilities" that an ounce or two of whiskey in the morning may be beneficial to people who have arrhythmia. Jake goes on to define arrhythmia as a condition where there is an abnormal heartbeat.

Well all due respect to Edwardsville as a capitol of medical knowledge (*umm*, have you been in Edwardsville lately?), it seems that Jake may be on to something. I did a fast Google search with the words arrhythmia and whiskey and darned if it doesn't seem like a couple of belts may in fact be a very good thing. Most of the information I came across suggested a couple of glasses of red wine were a good idea, but none said whiskey was necessarily bad. As long as it's no more then two drinks for woman a day, three for men the studies seem to indicate the Jake from Edwardsville was right.

But what about that morning part of the equation. Jake is right about the drinking but he has suggested, as he said, to leading research centers, that you start your day with Old Grand Dad. Now two shots of Jack Daniel's will not only put a big smile on my face but a whole new perspective on the day. Also a definite smell of booze on the breath.

I am trying to picture how to explain to my boss at an 8 a.m. meeting why I smell like that. "It's for my heart," I would say.

"Go home and sleep it off," he would probably say or maybe, "You're fired."

I am also thinking in my head about how you would imbibe those early morning pick-me-ups. Old Crow and Cheerios? Jameson's and juice? Wild Turkey and eggs? Somehow the idea of two straight shots of Johnnie Walker at 6 a.m. doesn't seem like something I could do. And don't forget I'm Irish.

Wait a minute. I am pretty sure there is a whisky called Early Times. What a brilliant marketing idea. Early Times for your early times. *Or then again I could be wrong.* Here's looking at you, Jake.

You see some interesting items at flea markets.

I have seen but not bought an actual World War II bomb, a bunch of coat racks made from deer hooves and of course the usual assorted guitars with one or two strings missing.

But only once in recent memory do I recall seeing a religious item like the tabernacle we saw the other day. For those of you who are not familiar with the Catholic faith the tabernacle houses the host or unleavened bread which the faithful believe is the body of Jesus Christ. It's a pretty important and holy part of any Catholic church and that's why it was a little surprising to find it among the used circular saws and dusty records at the flea market. I asked the vendor about it's origin but he was a little vague. Asking price for the tabernacle was $400.

What is perplexing to me is that you can actually buy something which so many held so sacred for so many years at such a place. Now I am far from being the most religious of men. I think I can still enter a church without being immediately struck by lighting or consumed by fire and I have never been chased by hostile nuns. But I have to believe all that would change if I brought the tabernacle home with me. First of all where to put it? Tossing it in the corner of the living room seems, well, a little crass. Wouldn't feel exactly right in the bedroom either, if you get my drift. Then comes the question of what to use it for. Wouldn't seem exactly right for a bread box, although that's sort of what it was.

The real issue here is that this sort of thing will become more and more available as churches are shuttered and the contents go on sale at flea markets and even on eBay. Priestly vestments, chalices and holy statues sold to the highest bidder or at a tag sale just doesn't feel right. But churches close every day as congregations dwindle and priests become scarce. In the past few years I know this area has seen many churches in small towns, like Larksville, Pennsylvania, locked up for good. Something has to be done with all the religious items and just taking them to the landfill doesn't seem like a solution either.

And what about the churches? My mom's brother was a priest. The building that was his church is now a small store. I am told where the altar was has become the meat counter. Are these all sign posts on the slippery slope to the warm place? I think so. *But then again I could be wrong.*

ABOUT THE AUTHOR

J im Rising is the Program Director of 102.3 The Mountain WDMT and hosts a weekday show called *Rising at Ten*. He plays what he wants and rants a bit. Jim lives with his "long suffering wife" Nancy in Dallas, Pennsylvania along with his lawn tractor and annoying neighbor. Feel free to email Jim at *rising@102themountain.com*.